THERE'S M...

PIZZA

CAROL HEDGES

Scripture Union
130 City Road, London EC1V 2NJ.

Other books by this author
Guardian Angel – *Impressions* series
Three's a Crowd – *Impressions* series
Ring of Silver, Lord of Time – *Leopard* series

© Carol Hedges 1995
First published 1995

ISBN 086201 921 4

British Library Cataloguing-in-Publication Data.
A catalogue record for this book is available from the British Library.

Phototypeset by Intype, London
Printed and bound in Great Britain by Cox & Wyman Ltd, Reading

~ 1 ~

Dear Diary,
  Today is Tuesday, January the first.
  The first day of the New Year.
  The beginning of the rest of my life.

Melissa paused. She looked out of her bedroom window. In the garden a few pathetic sparrows were hopping aimlessly around the empty flower beds. The sky was leaden grey and it was beginning to rain. Miserable weather, she thought gloomily. She turned back to her diary.

She wrote, *My New Year's resolutions are:*
  1. Help around house more often.
  2. Be nicer to Alex and Alice more often.
  3. Go to Christian Union more often.
  4. Do something about Steve Hayes.

She paused again. She looked at what she had written so far and sighed. Half way down page one and already she was running into output problems.

Funny how the idea of keeping a diary had seemed such a good one last term. They had read extracts from *The Diary of Anne Frank* in class, Mrs Hobson explaining how it was not only the personal story of a teenager growing up, but also an important historical record of Jewish life during the Nazi occupation of Holland. Just imagine, she had said, sweeping round the classroom and knocking things off people's desks, if future generations found *your* diary fifty years from now. What would it tell them about you and the world you lived in? And her steely glance had challenged them to take her up on the implied suggestion.

Back then, it had seemed like a great idea: keep a diary, write down all her secret thoughts and dreams, give posterity a real treat, but now, faced with all those empty white pages, Melissa began to have her doubts. What on earth was there to write about? Weather . . . boring. Life . . . boring. It wasn't really the sort of stuff that future generations would find totally riveting, was it? Anyway, nothing really exciting ever seemed to happen to her.

Not for the first time, Melissa wondered how on earth Anne Frank had managed to fill up all those pages to begin with. After all, she was considerably younger . . . thirteen was practically still at Junior school . . . and she never actually *went* anywhere interesting or met any new people. Mind you, she thought ruefully, re-reading her New Year's resolutions for the third time, if she seriously intended to keep some of them, she would probably have to spend the rest of her life shut up in her bedroom on her own, as well. Maybe she *was* being a little over ambitious!

Melissa closed the diary, locked it and placed it carefully in the back of her desk drawer. This was getting too much like hard work. Time for a little serious relaxation. She selected a tape from the rack, lay back on her bed and put on her headphones.

Future generations would just have to wait a bit longer.

'Melissa! . . . Melissa!!' her mum's voice interrupted the music.

What now? Melissa thought. 'Yeah?' she yelled, not bothering to remove the headphones.

'You promised to sort the washing out. Can you come down and do it?'

'I'm busy,' Melissa yelled. There was a significant pause.

'Now, please!' her mum shouted back.

Melissa sighed. Why couldn't she be left in peace? Grumbling to herself, she trailed over to the door, opened it, and nearly fell head over heels down the stairs. Directly outside was a large cardboard box and leading from it was a maze of kitchen rolls. The landing carpet was covered in paper shavings. Alice had been making another of her mega gerbil runs.

Melissa kicked the cardboard box angrily. For goodness sake, she thought, I could have broken my neck! 'Mum,' she called down, 'Alice is making a mess on the landing. I thought you said she wasn't to.'

Alice, who was ten, emerged from her bedroom carrying one of the gerbils. 'Telltale!' she exclaimed.

Melissa's mother came up the stairs and surveyed the appalling chaos on the carpet. She groaned. 'Tidy it all up, Alice,' she said wearily, 'and then *you*,' she added, looking at Melissa, 'can run the hoover over it — after you've sorted the washing.'

'Pigging slave-driver,' Melissa muttered, very softly so that her mum wouldn't hear, but of course she did.

'Oh really?' her mum said, acidly, 'So you think you're being overworked, do you? Let me tell you something, my little ray of sunshine, you lot couldn't survive five minutes on your own. You'd just better hope the day never comes when I'm not here to cook for you and clean up after all of you!'

'Yeah . . . yeah,' Melissa said, to keep the peace. Her mum often droned on like this. 'Planning on going off to the Bahamas, are you?' she added, cheekily.

Her mum shot her a beady look. 'Washing,' she said grimly, 'and hoovering.' She turned and stalked back downstairs.

Alice began to pile the cardboard tubes back into the box. She was quivering and red-faced with indignation. 'Sneak!' she hissed. 'Dobber!'

'Just get on with it, Alice,' Melissa told her. Alice looked up at her and stuck out her tongue. 'Or . . .,' Melissa continued, bringing her face to within a couple of inches of her sister's face, 'I shall take your stupid gerbils and feed them to the *cat*!!'

This was the worst threat she could utter. Alice gasped in horror and began tidying up at high speed. Melissa watched her for a few seconds, and then sauntered slowly downstairs trying not to mind that she'd broken two of her resolutions already!

The Customer Services Desk in Marks and Spencer was rushed off its feet. It seemed like everybody in the world was exchanging unwanted Christmas presents. The queue stretched three deep right through the shop as far as the food-hall. Melissa sighed and pulled a face as she attached herself to the back. It was really depressing. All those people who had cheerfully gone shopping before Christmas and bought presents for their family and friends, and now, the family and friends were all back returning them.

When her turn finally came, Melissa handed over the red woollen gloves (Aunt Jen), the green paisley shawl (Gran, who seemed to have forgotten that she was fifteen not fifty!), and the box of matching talc and bath oil (Mum's friend from church).

'Cash or credit?' asked the tired girl behind the counter listlessly.

'Cash please,' Melissa replied.

She intended spending the money on some badly needed folders for school. But, as luck would have it, she happened to see a long-sleeved man's pullover in the sale, just as she was leaving the shop. It was big, which was good. And it was black, which was better, because black was *the* colour to be wearing just now. It would also go nicely with the long print skirt that she had seen in her mate Caron's mum's catalogue. And it was reduced by so much that she simply couldn't leave it there, could she? After all, school files could be bought any old day, but a bargain had to be snapped up at once!

That evening, Melissa decided to try out her new jumper on the rest of the family. She changed out of her jeans into a pair of black leggings, tied her hair back with a black and silver velvet scrunch, and put on the jumper. It looked fantastic!

She went into the bathroom and peered at herself in the mirror. Time to Blitz those Zits with new Zitsbuster (as advertised on TV). It was new! It was revolutionary! It was also bright green and smelt like lavatory cleaner, but who cared? She squeezed a little out onto a piece of cotton wool and wiped it over her forehead, nose and chin.

Actually, Melissa didn't really need to blitz her zits because her complexion was practically flawless. And her hair, which was brown with golden highlights, hung in curls down to her shoulders. Other girls only achieved hair like hers after much backcombing in the girls' toilets. She also had large brown eyes with long sweeping eyelashes, and she never seemed to put on any weight, no matter how much junk food she ate.

Yes, all things considered, Melissa was secretly very pleased with her appearance. She knew she looked pretty OK. But of course, it would never do to admit it publicly. That was asking for trouble. So she dutifully moaned and complained just like everybody else and made out that she was much too fat, had far too many spots, was a complete mess and generally looked terrible. It did not do to get a reputation. Particularly if you were supposed to be a Christian. That was trouble enough!

She sauntered downstairs. Her mum was in the kitchen lifting a large casserole out of the oven, which was something she was not meant to do with her bad back. She straightened up and surveyed Melissa thoughtfully.

'Is that a new jumper?' she asked. Then added, 'Isn't it a bit . . . big?' She peered at Melissa's face, 'And are you feeling all right? You look a funny colour to me.'

Melissa sniffed indignantly and went into the living room, where Alex and Alice were playing a quarrelsome game of Ludo on the rug. Games with Alice always ended in rows because she still cheated.

Their dad looked up from a giant Christmas crossword that he was still trying to complete.

'Is that one of my sweaters?' he inquired, vaguely.

'No, Dad,' Melissa replied patiently.

Alex surveyed his sister. He was nineteen and Into Girls, but he liked them well dressed. Melissa was a constant source of disappointment.

'You look like a walking funeral,' he told her disapprovingly.

Alice took one look and went, 'Yuk!'

Mewcus the cat got up from the hearth-rug and

left the room, carefully skirting round Melissa's ankles, which he regarded with disgust. Typical, Melissa thought to herself. No appreciation at all. Why did she bother?

'Tea,' Mum called from the kitchen.

Alex unfolded himself from the carpet and glanced at his watch.

'Not for me, Mum,' he said, heading for the door, 'I'm out of here.'

'So who is it tonight?' Melissa inquired sarcastically, 'Still Kathryn, or have you moved on?'

Alex went through girlfriends like some girls went through tights. It was because he was so tall, with the same curly brown hair and brown eyes that Melissa had. It was an irresistible combination as far as the female sex was concerned. Alex had had girls falling over themselves to get near him ever since he was in the Infants, and now he was at college and had his own transport, he was even more irresistible. No youth group was safe!

'Still Kathryn,' he grinned.

'That's three whole weeks,' Melissa remarked, as the rest of the family sat down at the kitchen table. 'He must be in love!'

'Hi gorgeous!'

Melissa turned round quickly. She was feeling anything but gorgeous. It was the first day of term. It was lashing down with rain and she had managed to ladder her tights on the way to school. The comment came from one of the sixth formers who was on gate duty. Melissa recognised him at once. Well, let's face it, she thought, who didn't? It was Justin Adams, star of the school basketball team, ace footballer and regarded generally as drop-dead gorgeous. He was tall and dark-haired with deep blue eyes and there were several girls in her class who just *died* every time they saw him.

Melissa lowered her eyes and smiled demurely back at him. So Justin Adams thought she was gorgeous, did he? Maybe life was not so bad after all.

She made her way over to the Year Eleven block, keeping an eye out for Steve, but as usual, he was nowhere to be seen. Probably waiting until the last minute to put in an appearance, she thought to herself, that is, if he was coming in at all. She knew if she wanted to talk to him, she'd have to get to him whilst he was on his own. Steve didn't speak to her when he was with his mates. Not that he spoke much to her when he was on his own either, Melissa reflected, so why was she bothering?

Melissa went into her form room. As expected, all the girls were sitting on each other's desks, comparing notes about Christmas and showing off their new bracelets and watches. The boys were talking football and computers and everybody was ignoring Darren Davy and Jason Marshall who were creating their own little charisma-free area over by the radiators.

Melissa glanced round. Her best friend Melanie hadn't arrived yet. Pity. So she slung herself onto a desk and joined in the general discussion about the sheer awfulness of Christmas, and the stuffiness of parents and how you never got the presents you really wanted!

'Hiya Melissa,' Melanie Pearson dumped her bag on her desk and perched herself on the edge. 'Did you have a good Christmas?'

'The pits,' Melissa told her cheerfully. 'You?'

'Actually, it was great,' Melanie told her enthusiastically. 'We went to stay with Gran and Gramps in the country. My cousins came too. It was really special.

All the family going to church together on Christmas Day.'

'Well, lucky old you,' one of the girls sneered sarcastically, 'sounds like a real barrel of laughs!'

'Yeah,' someone else put in, 'Christmas is mega boring. Too much fattening food.'

'Having to be polite to all those wrinklies.'

'Stupid prezzies.'

Melanie looked round at the hard cynical faces and Melissa groaned inwardly. She knew what was coming. Melanie was about to put them right about Christmas.

'But that's not the *real* Christmas,' Melanie said, her glance travelling round the group. Her blue eyes gleamed behind her glasses. 'Christmas is about the birth of Christ. It's about God becoming a man. The food and presents bit has nothing to do with the real meaning of Christmas.'

'Yeah . . . yeah . . . right on, Melanie,' yawned one of the girls, exchanging amused glances with her friends. 'If you say so . . .'

The classroom door opened and Mrs Hobson strode in, piled high with textbooks. The groups of girls scattered and dived for their desks.

Melanie eased herself off her desk and sat down. She took out her notebook and biro. Then she turned round to Melissa who sat behind her.

'Why didn't *you* tell them about Christmas?' she whispered accusingly.

Melissa sighed. Sometimes . . . no, to be honest, most of the time, Melanie managed to make her feel totally inadequate.

'Er . . . I was just going to when you arrived,' she lied bravely.

'Right!' Mrs Hobson barked, standing up and closing the register, 'Eyes *front*!'

Mrs Hobson taught GCSE English and coached the girls' netball team in her spare time. She was very tall with immensely wide shoulders and always wore a tweed suit, thick fawn tights and brown lace-up brogues. It was rumoured that in the past, she had received SAS training. She was commonly known as The Rottweiler in a Skirt.

'I'm sure I don't have to tell you,' Mrs Hobson boomed, prowling up and down the aisles and slapping battered copies of *Macbeth* onto everyone's desk as she passed, 'that in a few months from now you will all be sitting your GCSE exams. It is a crucial time in your educative process. And may I remind you all that I Can't Do The Work For You.'

Everybody's lips moved in time with her words. They knew it off by heart. They had heard it all before. Many, many times. Suddenly, Mrs Hobson came to a halt in front of Darren's desk. She stiffened.

'What is that object dangling from your left earlobe, Darren?' she inquired icily.

Darren smirked. 'It's an earring, Miss,' he said.

'Not in my class, it isn't! Take it off at once. You know the school rules!'

'But Miss,' Darren protested innocently, 'William Shakespeare wore an earring. I saw a picture of him in a library book, and he definitely had an earring on.'

Darren's mates sniggered delightedly. Good old Daz! Trust him to give The Hogsbum a hard time. Mrs Hobson drew herself up to her full height, which from where Melissa was sitting looked to be about eight feet.

'Darren, there are three major differences between you and William Shakespeare,' she informed him acidly. 'One: Shakespeare wrote plays. You do not.

12

Two: Shakespeare was famous. You are not. Three: Shakespeare has been dead for three hundred years. You, alas are still very much alive. Although if you do not remove that earring *now*, I cannot guarantee that you will be alive for much longer!'

Everyone laughed and Darren removed the earring, scowling and muttering under his breath. Mrs Hobson gave a viperish smile.

'Thank you so much. And now, if playtime is over, let us get back to work. *Macbeth*, act two, scene three . . . Caron, perhaps you would like to read from line one?'

Melissa sighed. Nine-thirty on the first morning of term and already she felt as if she had been sitting there for ever.

~ 2 ~

It was Tuesday lunch time and Melissa did not know why she had this strange, uncontrollable urge to go home. There was no earthly reason why she should be out of school. It was two weeks into the term, she had her work well under control (fairly well under control) and normally at twelve-thirty she would have been in the canteen with her mates queuing for lunch. (Stodge and chips, followed by stodge and custard, followed by acute indigestion.)

All she knew was that from the moment she arrived at the school gate, she had had an uneasy feeling that she ought to turn straight around and go back home. She had tried to dismiss the feeling – it was double French – enough to make anyone think of escaping. But throughout the morning, the feeling had persisted and grown stronger – which was why she was now hurrying down the street, her coat slung over her shoulders and her heart hammering in a strange and frightening way. And just to make matters worse, she had left school without obtaining an exit pass from the School Office, which meant that she would be in very serious trouble if anybody spotted her.

Everything had seemed totally normal when she left home that morning. Alice had mislaid her gym bag for the billionth time. Alex had overslept. Dad had left at the crack of dawn to drive to Birmingham for a three day conference and Mum was threatening another massive cleaning raid on all their bedrooms. A perfectly normal morning in the White household, Melissa thought, as her feet carried her at top speed up the front path. So why all this urgency to get home? She pulled her key out of her bag and unlocked the front door. Dropping her bag on the floor, she stood in the hallway, and sniffed. No smell of smoke, so that obviously wasn't the reason, thank goodness.

'Mum,' she called, 'where are you?'

'Up here,' came the muffled reply.

Melissa pounded up the stairs. The voice seemed to be coming from her room. She pushed open the door. Her mother was lying face down on the carpet, surrounded by an untidy heap of Melissa's clean clothes. She tried to raise her shoulders and twist round to see her, but winced as a wave of pain hit her and lay back down again, her face contorted in agony.

'Mum!' Melissa knelt down next to her. 'What's happened?'

'My back went,' her mum replied with a groan. 'I was just reaching forward to pull out one of your drawers so that I could put those clean clothes in and it went into spasm. I think it's probably serious this time, Mel. Can you phone the doctor? I can't get to the phone – I just can't seem to move my legs at all.'

'Oh Mum,' Melissa's eyes filled with tears. The thought of her mother lying all alone on the bedroom floor in pain was too awful to contemplate. She also remembered guiltily, that she had meant to take that pile of clean clothes upstairs and put them away herself.

But, of course, she had forgotten.

'You could have been here all day!' she exclaimed.

'Maybe,' her mum agreed. 'Though I *did* pray for someone to come round.' She gave Melissa a brave smile, 'And look what happened – you arrived out of the blue.'

So that was why I kept feeling like I had to go home, Melissa thought. Weird!

'Can I do anything for you?' she asked the prone figure on the floor.

'Cup of tea?' her mother suggested, hopefully. 'I've been dying for one since nine o'clock. You could put the kettle on after you've rung the surgery.'

She tried to turn over onto her side, but gave up after a few minutes' struggle and returned to lying flat on the floor.

'Don't you ever clean under your bed?' she remarked. 'It's absolutely disgusting under here!'

'Hospital?' Alice wailed. 'Is she going to die?'

'Hospital?' Alex asked. 'Who's doing the cooking?'

It was four o'clock, but it seemed to Melissa that a week had gone by. She had phoned the doctor, who in turn had phoned the hospital, which had sent an ambulance to take Mum to the big new hospital on the outskirts of the town.

At three-thirty, Melanie had called round with the folders that Melissa had left on her desk and a list of the homework they had been given. 'Traction?' she had asked. 'What's that?'

'It means she has to lie flat, with weights hung onto her legs, I think,' Melissa told her. 'And then they

16

might let her come home. Or they may operate and take a disc out. Whatever, she's likely to be in hospital for a good six to eight weeks, the doctor said.'

'Wow!' Melanie's eyes rounded in amazement. 'All that just for opening a drawer!'

'It's not the first time,' Melissa said. 'She knows she has to be careful, but she doesn't take any notice. We try to help but she always ends up doing the wrong things.'

But you didn't help this time, did you? her conscience reminded her.

'So how are you going to manage without her?' Melanie asked.

'Don't know. I guess we'll all have to do our bit,' Melissa said, vaguely. Somehow she hadn't got round to thinking about life without Mum. It was scary enough watching that ambulance pulling away from the house, with all the curtains in the street twitching.

'You'll be OK,' Melanie reassured her, 'once word gets round your church, everyone will offer to help, won't they? That's what being a Christian is all about.'

Yes Melanie, anything you say Melanie, Melissa thought, trying to find comfort in her words. I am not panicking! she told herself firmly. There was something very . . . final about ambulances.

After Melanie had gone, Melissa went to the freezer. She found some shepherd's pie and an apple crumble. She decided to throw them into the microwave for supper. Then she rang Birmingham and left a message for her dad. Tomorrow . . . but she wouldn't worry about tomorrow, she decided. Melanie was probably right. People would help them out. They'd better, she thought ruefully. Somehow she just couldn't see Alex in the kitchen and it wouldn't be fair to expect Dad to cook after a long drive from the office. As for Alice, Melissa shuddered. Anyone with fingernails that filthy was a walking health hazard! No, if she wasn't careful she could just see herself being lumbered with the lot – cooking, cleaning and shopping, on top of school work and everything else in her life.

Melissa sat at the kitchen table nursing a Coke and trying to make sense of what had happened. Why me, God? she found herself asking and almost immediately she recalled what she had written in her diary only a couple of weeks ago. Then she remembered her mum saying that she didn't think they could cope without her. So this was a kind of test, was it? God taking her at her word. All at once, Melissa felt slightly more confident. She could cope. They would manage. After all, God wouldn't let them starve. He would help them out.

Trust and obey, that was the answer, even though it went against the grain – Melissa liked to feel she was in control herself, and she also liked to be the one giving out the orders but maybe, in this case, she was just going to have to grit her teeth and get on with it!

The microwave pinged and Melissa took out the shepherd's pie and set it on the table. 'Mum's going to be fine,' she told Alice reassuringly, 'just a few weeks in hospital, and she'll be good as new. Alex will drive us over to see her straight after tea.'

'But . . .' began Alex.

'Yes, you will!' Melissa snapped.

'Yeah, OK,' Alex agreed. One look at his sister's face told him that resistance was not only useless but potentially fatal. 'Just let me make a couple of phone calls first.'

'Leave some pie for Dad,' Melissa told them both.

'He'll be in later.'

'You're beginning to sound like Mum already,' Alex commented disapprovingly.

'Yes well, someone has got to take control round here,' Melissa said.

'Why should it be you?' Alex asked, wolfing down his dinner as if it was his last meal on earth.

'Think about it for a minute,' Melissa said. 'What's the alternative? If we don't get ourselves organised quickly, Dad might invite Gran over to look after us.'

'Aaargghhh!' Alice shrieked. 'Not Gran!'

'Yeah, take your point, Mel,' Alex agreed. 'Anything but Gran!'

'So if *we* decide we can cope,' Melissa said, stressing the 'we', 'then maybe we could quickly get a rota going for the cleaning and washing and stuff, and then we can present him with a . . .,' her mind struggled to remember the phrase they'd learned in French only the other week, 'a *fait accompli* . . . agreed?'

'Agreed,' Alice said. 'I don't mind helping.'

'Cleaning,' Alex murmured thoughtfully, 'and *washing*?'

'It's quite easy,' Melissa told him briskly. 'You put all the dirty clothes into that big white machine with the glass door, in the utility room. I'll introduce you to it later. Anyway, we should be OK for food. People from church are bound to help out.'

'Perhaps they could do the cleaning and washing too?' Alex suggested, getting up and ignoring Melissa's despairing look. 'Phone calls,' he said, disappearing into the hall.

'He's useless, isn't he?' Alice remarked cheerfully.

'Totally. I don't know what any self-respecting girl sees in him,' Melissa agreed.

'I really think we should phone Gran.'

Melissa's father had had tea, been to the hospital and was now holding a family discussion round the kitchen table. 'Six to eight weeks is a long time to manage on our own.'

'We'll be fine Dad, don't get stressed out,' Alex said. 'Mel's got it all under control. She's done a rota.'

'Fake a crumbly,' Alice added. Their dad looked a bit puzzled.

'Anyway, Gran's bound to be busy,' Melissa put in quickly.

'And you know she's allergic to cats,' Alice said, stroking Mewcus, 'and to gerbils.'

'And house dust.'

'And practically everything else.'

Their father sighed, resignedly. 'Well, maybe we'll give it a week or so and see how we all get on.'

'Great stuff, Dad,' Melissa smiled. 'After all, you're always saying we should be more responsible. So now's our chance.'

The phone rang. 'I'll get it,' their father said. He pushed back his chair and went out of the kitchen.

Melissa gave the other two a triumphant thumbs up sign.

'That was Melanie's mother,' he said, coming back two minutes later. 'She says she's sorry to hear about Mum and she'll bring something round for tomorrow's tea later on tonight.'

'There you are, Dad,' Melissa told him, sending up a quick 'thank-you' to God, 'I told you, we're all going to be fine.'

Melissa White and Melanie Pearson had been friends for a couple of years. Ever since Year Eight when Melanie's family moved to the area and she had started at Melissa's school. They were the only two Christians in the class, which gave them something in common at once. Collectively, they were known as the Two Mels, (or the Two Smells if you listened to Darren and his friends).

It seemed on the surface an unlikely friendship. Melissa was pretty, self-assured and had a rather slap-dash attitude to life in general. By contrast, Melanie was serious and a bit intense. She wore her long fair hair scraped back in a plait, and her blue eyes were well hidden behind large round glasses. She looked like the sort of girl who featured in one of those 'before and after' beauty articles in the magazines. Except that Melanie had never advanced beyond the 'before' stage.

There were other differences too – Melissa's Christianity was quite definitely of the 'could do better' variety, and depended a lot upon how she was feeling at the time. She knew she ought to talk to her friends about God when she got a chance, but she rarely did, principally because she enjoyed being popular and hated getting into trouble. She always regretted it later. She was also quick-tempered and inclined to speak first and think later and, as Alex was never tired of pointing out, if they ever made jumping to conclusions an Olympic sport, Melissa could do it for England. Her family went to the local Baptist church which was small and friendly but didn't have many teenagers in it.

Melanie's family, on the other hand, went to a Fellowship, which was another word for a house church that had got too big for its house and migrated to a local school. It was a big Fellowship, with its own minibus. All the youth group wore yellow T-shirts with the words, Mustard Seed Fellowship: The

Church For Today's People printed on them and were often featured in the local paper as they did a lot of work for charity and raised enormous sums of money by sponsored pray-ins and other activities. Melanie never missed an opportunity to talk about her beliefs. She also knew her way around the Bible much better than Melissa did and so was always able to back up what she said with a relevant quote. Melissa had reached the conclusion quite early on in their relationship that Melanie belonged to the 'When-the-going-gets-tough-the-tough-get-quoting' school of faith. Also, she never wavered in her beliefs, unlike Melissa, who, if she was honest had to admit to herself that she occasionally had doubts, especially after she had spent a lot of time with her non-Christian mates, who all seemed to get along quite nicely without going to church or spending time reading the Bible and praying each morning.

Melissa knew that her parents approved of Melanie and thought that she was a very good influence on her. She wasn't sure quite what Melanie's parents thought about her, so when the Pearson's car drew up at the gate later that evening, and Melanie's mum got out, carefully carrying two covered dishes, Melissa put on her nicest smile as she opened the door.

'Hello, Melissa dear,' Anne Pearson greeted her. She was wearing a long flowered dress, and her hair was tucked away under a headscarf. 'How is your mother?'

'She's not too bad, thank you very much, Mrs Pearson,' Melissa replied politely. 'Would you like to come in?'

'No thank you, dear. I'm just on my way to a church meeting.' Melanie's mother smiled encouragingly and handed over the two dishes. 'Shepherd's pie and an apple crumble,' she said. 'You only need to heat them

22

up. Well, please tell your mother that we shall all be praying for her, won't you?'

'Er . . . yes of course I will. Thanks.' Melissa stood awkwardly at the door, balancing the two dishes and watching as Mrs Pearson drove off.

Oh well, she thought, taking the food into the kitchen, mustn't grumble. As Mum always says, 'There's more to life than pizza'.

She put the dishes down on the work surface and decided to tackle the washing-up. Dad had retired into his study and she could hear his computer chuntering happily. Alice was probably upstairs giving her gerbils some exercise. And Alex? Who knows, she thought, he could be anywhere. It was funny how people vanished whenever there was any work to be done, she thought to herself grimly, as she filled the sink with hot water. She remembered Mum saying something along the same lines, too.

Not for the first time, Melissa was struck by the way washing-up always seemed such *fun* on TV with small kids asking cute questions about the softness of your hands and dishes miraculously appearing in the plate rack sparkling clean. Trouble was, the reality tended to fall rather short. It took her nearly a whole hour to wash, dry and tidy away all the tea things – an hour that she could have spent doing homework, she thought virtuously, even though she knew she would probably have spent it listening to a tape.

Well, at least we've got some tea for tomorrow, she reminded herself, trying to look on the bright side. Even if it *was* exactly the same meal that they had just eaten, and it was only another six weeks or so until Mum came home, she thought. Six rather long weeks.

But they were all going to cope admirably. Weren't they?

~ 3 ~

The changing room windows were all wet and steamy. Little rivulets of water were running down onto the sill. The air was cold and smelt of perspiration and talcum powder. Melissa shivered, wrinkling her nose with disgust. There were piles of discarded clothes everywhere, on the benches and strewn with careless abandon all over the floor.

It was quite obvious that nobody in her class had ever had to do their own ironing, she thought, stripping off her school uniform and hanging it up carefully on a peg. It was a funny thing, but ever since her mother had gone into hospital two weeks ago, and she had been left in sole charge of the family ironing, for the first time in her life Melissa had found herself carefully hanging things up and putting things away tidily. Which was a lot more than could be said for the rest of her class! Honestly, she thought, it looked as if a bomb had hit the changing rooms.

Melissa dived into her aertex games shirt, her arms covered with goosebumps. If it was cold in here, she thought with a shiver, then what on earth was it going to be like outside on the hockey field? She put on her school jumper, two pairs of tights and a pair of Alex's rugby socks followed by her tracksuit bottoms. She was still cold. She peered hopefully into the Lost Property basket, even though she knew that the rest of her class had raided it five minutes before her arrival. Melissa had had to stay behind and explain to Mrs Hobson that Alice's gerbils had made a midnight snack out of her English homework.

The only thing now left in the basket was an old woolly cardigan with most of the buttons missing. Better than nothing at all, she decided, fishing it out and slipping her arms into the sleeves. She put her tracksuit top over the cardigan. It was getting difficult to bend her arms as she had so many layers of clothing on. She felt as if she was taking part in one of those stupid kids' party games. She peered into the steamed up mirror. What a mess! It was always the same, on Wednesday afternoons. A mad scramble to get into as many layers of clothing as quickly as possible before charging out onto the freezing pitch for an hour's torture. By the end of the afternoon, her face would be red and raw from the biting wind, and her confidence totally destroyed by the sarcastic comments of Mrs Ashton, the games teacher.

Not for the first time, Melissa wondered whether there mightn't be some law somewhere against such cruelty. She thought enviously of her two friends, Caron Smith and Aimee Johnston, who were working in the library. They were not coming out to hockey, lucky things, because they had got their periods. Actually, this was their third period in five weeks. Mrs Ashton still hadn't realised what was going on. It was grossly unfair! How come honest girls like herself were forced to suffer the indignities and torture of an afternoon's hockey, she thought to herself, whilst cunning skivers like those two were sitting in a warm library reading *Just Seventeen* behind their history text-books? And it wasn't even as if she had Melanie to moan at, for Melanie was at home with a bad cold. Life was full of injustice, Melissa decided, and she *was* always the one who got dumped on.

Then suddenly she remembered something and her lips curved into a secret smile. Maybe she *was* just about to launch herself out into the freezing cold world and yeah, she resented the way Caron and Aimee always got away with it, but she had something that they would have *died* for. She had a note from Justin Adams actually asking her out on a date!

He had given it to her that morning at the school gate. He was on prefect duty again and Melissa had stopped to chat with him for a bit, as she always did now. They had talked for a few minutes about nothing much and then, just as she turned to go in through the gate, Justin had slipped the note into her hand, smiled his devastatingly wonderful smile and walked away. It had all happened so suddenly that Melissa was through the gate and half way up the path before she realised what he had done.

She had rushed into the girls' toilets, locked herself into a cubicle, and ripped open the envelope.

Dear Melissa, she read, *Would you like to go out with me on Saturday? Justin.*

For a few seconds, Melissa had stared down at the spiky writing, scarcely able to breathe. Her heart was beating like mad and she felt her cheeks going scarlet, even though there was nobody else there. Dear Melissa . . . a date . . . Justin Adams fancied her!!! The boy whose name featured on more pencil cases than the latest pop star had actually asked *her* to go out with him! It was so utterly mega-fantastic that for a moment, she thought she might faint! Just wait until Melanie hears about this, she had thought gleefully, she is going to be so *amazed* she won't know what to say!

Oh yes she will. Melissa came down to earth with a bump. She knew just what Melanie was going to say. Melanie was going to say that she shouldn't go out with gorgeous, hunky Justin because he wasn't a Christian. And she would probably find some bit in the Bible to back her up. And she would go on and on endlessly about it until she had worn Melissa down and made her promise to say no to him. Well, one thing was for sure, she was going to have to keep it a secret from Melanie. And that meant from everyone else in her class too, or someone was bound to split.

Melissa had refolded the note and placed it reverently between the covers of her maths book. Bother Melanie, she thought. There were times when she could be such a killjoy! After all, it wasn't as if she was going to *marry* Justin Adams, they were only going out as friends. Anyway, she reasoned to herself, Alex went out with lots of girls and who was to say that they were all Christians, even though he said they were. Well, maybe some of them weren't. So why shouldn't she go out with Justin? And anyway, she thought, maybe if Justin went out with her, then she could invite him to come along to the Christian Union and then, in time maybe even to church.

There was a knock on the toilet door. 'Are you OK?' someone shouted.

'Yeah,' Melissa unlocked the door. A sixth form girl was standing outside, looking worried. 'You've been in there ages!' she said, disapprovingly.

'Umm . . . I'm just going,' Melissa replied dreamily.

As she ran out to join the rest of her class, Melissa went over the events of the day yet again. It felt great to know that someone thought she was special and that she had been asked out by the best looking, most popular boy in the school. Not that she had finally decided whether she *was* going out with him, yet. After all, it didn't do to appear too keen. Well, she had sort of decided. It was only that nagging little voice in her head that was making her hold back. But with a bit of luck, an hour's hockey in the raw freezing world outside would silence the voice completely.

There was no doubt about it, the house was a bit of a tip. Someone had forgotten to empty the waste-baskets yet again and there was a pile of dirty washing in front of the washing machine. Melissa consulted the rota pinned to the kitchen notice board — Alex. Of course, she might have guessed. And where was her brother now? Probably out with his latest girl-friend, whose name escaped her. Honestly, she gave up!

'Melissa?' Alice appeared at the top of the stairs, holding one of her gerbils, 'I've hoovered the lounge and put the dinner in the oven.'

'Great stuff,' Melissa smiled up at her. At least some-one is pulling their weight around here, she thought.

She went into the lounge to inspect Alice's efforts. Everything was tidy — videos stacked neatly under the TV and the magazines in a pile on the coffee table. Good old Alice. She mustn't forget to make it up to her when Mum came home. Then she noticed the carpet. She looked, frowned and looked again. You could see exactly where Alice had gone — up and down, up and down, in stripes. She must have leaned rather heavily on the hoover as well. It made the carpet look . . . mown. Oh well, Melissa decided, shrugging her shoulders, it was probably best not to notice. She had far too many other things to worry about than a lounge carpet that now bore a distinct resemblance to the centre court at Wimbledon.

Melissa went into the kitchen and peered into the oven. Surprise, surprise — shepherd's pie and apple crumble again. It appeared to be the only thing people in church could cook. Fortunately no one in the family seemed to have noticed their slightly monotonous diet. Alex always ate as fast as possible as he was inevitably on his way out somewhere, and Alice would have eaten shepherd's bootlaces so long as they were covered in tomato ketchup and their dad was too preoccupied with work and visiting their mother to notice what he was eating. Anyway, it was only a couple more weeks and Mum would be back home, Melissa reminded herself.

Visions of lasagne and beef casserole rose mouthwateringly before her eyes. Funny how she had never properly appreciated her mum's cooking before now. And the way she managed to keep the whole house clean — especially the bathroom. Melissa had to admit it, the bathroom had defeated her. She kept on spraying it with cleaner just like the glamorous model on TV with her wide smile and long red fingernails, but somehow the finished result did not entirely match up to the advert's promise. The bathroom looked smeary and dull instead of bright and sparkling and once, when she had casually run her finger across one of the surfaces (just like the model did) it had come away with a layer of dried foam.

Still, not long now until the weekend, she reminded

herself cheerfully as she set the table for tea, and then it would be time for her big date with Justin, (if she decided to go, of course).

Melissa still hadn't really seen Steve Hayes to talk to. They didn't seem to be in the same set for anything this term. She had caught fleeting glimpses of him in the corridor, as he slouched along, always wearing his 'lucky' green baseball cap but either he was on the move somewhere, or else she was surrounded by her own friends. However, she hadn't forgotten her New Year's resolution, and so when she spotted him in the canteen, she decided to make contact.

Steering a path between the groups of kids hunched around the dining tables, she called out gaily, 'Hi Steve, how're you doing?' as she passed his table. But as soon as she opened her mouth, she realised her mistake. Steve was sitting with a couple of his mates – whom she hadn't noticed.

He stared up at her, brushing his hair back from his forehead, his eyes hostile and wary.

'Pig off!' he snapped.

Affronted, Melissa walked on by and took her tray over to where her own friends were sitting. They, of course, had witnessed and heard the whole thing.

'Wasting your time there,' one girl remarked with a supercilious smile.

'Yeah, I don't know why you're throwing yourself at that creep,' remarked another. 'He's a total waste of space, if you ask me.'

'But he used to be different,' Melissa murmured.

She glanced over to where Steve sat. His two friends were going 'Hi Steve!' in false, sing-song voices and sniggering whilst Steve looked down at his plate, a hard, stony expression on his face.

In spite of herself, Melissa felt her eyes filling with tears. What had happened to him? They used to be such good mates back in the old days. She and Steve had gone to the same Junior school. They had both come up through Junior church together. Melissa could clearly remember the time when Steve used to come to church every Sunday, even though his parents never ever came with him, except for Christmas and Easter. And then, when they were in the top Juniors, they used to hang out together in the disused bus shelter down Westfield Road, laughing and chatting. You could talk to Steve about anything, in those days. He was a good listener with a great sense of humour and they both got on really well. Sometimes, Melissa thought, Steve was like a brother – no, better than a brother. She never fought with him the way she did with Alex.

Then suddenly, as soon as they both went into Year Eight, things seemed to fall apart and Steve stopped going around with her, and occasionally didn't come to church. Now, he went out of his way to avoid her, or so it seemed. And he never came near the church either. It was as if he just didn't want to know her or God.

Melissa knew that it had something to do with the gang of boys Steve was going around with. They were considerably older than he was and came mainly from the big Comprehensive over on the estate nearby. She had seen some of them hanging around the gate at three-thirty waiting for him and his mates to come out of school. They all swore a lot and most of them smoked. She had also spotted him with them one Saturday in town hanging around the seats outside Boots. They were all dressed alike – black jeans, shiny baseball jackets and baseball caps worn back to front and she thought that she saw Steve with a cigarette too, although afterwards, she wasn't absolutely sure about that.

All afternoon, the encounter with Steve returned to bug Melissa. Her pride had taken a knock and she had been made to look silly in front of her friends, who obviously thought she was trying unsuccessfully, to get off with him. As the afternoon went on however, she found that her feelings changed from embarrassment to anger. How dare he humiliate her like that, she fumed inwardly. Who did he think he was? If that was how he was going to react, then clearly he wasn't worth bothering about. He had made his own choices and he could go to hell as far as she was concerned!

All at once, a vision of Justin Adams swam before her, his blue eyes looking deep into hers, and his bewitching smile captivating her heart. Justin cared for her. He thought she was wonderful.

Suddenly, Melissa made up her mind. She would go out with him, after all. Why not? After all, what had she possibly got to lose?

She decided she would find him and tell him straight after school. It was going to be great going out with somebody who really appreciated her, she thought to herself. Just great. And with a bit of luck, neither Melanie nor her parents would ever find out.

~ 4 ~

It was Saturday. The day of Melissa's big date. She spent the morning catching up on homework as she had arranged to meet Melanie after lunch for a wander round the shops. It was their favourite way of spending Saturday afternoons, and normally, Melissa looked forward to wasting a couple of hours doing nothing much, but today, she couldn't help feeling slightly edgy. She kept glancing surreptitiously at her watch as the two of them drifted down the high street, peering into shop windows. Time passed so slowly when you were waiting for something to happen. It was ages until seven-thirty.

'Come on,' Melissa grabbed Melanie by the arm, and dragged her into Boots, 'let's go and try on perfume.'

They elbowed their way through the throngs of Saturday shoppers until they got to the perfume counter, where Melissa, after a quick glance round, selected a bottle of expensive looking scent from the samples display at the front of the counter. She sprayed it

33

liberally onto her wrists, waved her arms up and down for a few minutes and then sniffed.

'Quite nice,' she pronounced, in a posh voice, 'although I think it's a *little* bit heavy, don't you agree?'

Melanie giggled uncertainly. She wasn't into all this sophisticated chat. She wasn't really into expensive and powerful perfumes either – bubble-bath at Christmas and on her birthday, that was about as far as she preferred to go.

'Go on, Lanie, try this one,' Melissa picked up another bottle, labelled *Chant d'Amour*. She seized Melanie's wrist and gave the top of the bottle a squeeze. A fine jet of amber-coloured liquid shot out, filling the air around them with a pungent aroma.

'Pooh what a pong!' Melissa wrinkled her nose in disgust. 'Smells more like Chant du cat!'

Melanie raised her wrist to her face and took a cautious sniff. Melissa was quite right. It smelt horrible!

'Oh dear,' she said ruefully, 'I don't think I'd better try anything else. In fact, I'll have to wash this off before I go home. Mum and Dad will go spare if I come in smelling like this!'

'Don't fret,' Melissa told her reassuringly. 'It'll probably have worn off completely by the time you get home. Come on, let's try the eye-shadows now.'

They headed towards the make-up counter, Melanie trying to keep her arms pressed closely against her sides so that nobody would notice how vile she smelt. She wished she hadn't let Melissa spray her with perfume. She was sure she was going to get into trouble.

'Look,' Melissa suddenly hissed, clutching her by the arm, 'there's Carly Salter at the make-up counter. What a mess!'

Carly Salter was in the sixth form. She had very long black hair and a sharp, foxy face. She was nearly six foot tall and incredibly thin. You couldn't help noticing her. It was something about the way she sauntered along the corridor, always surrounded by a devoted crowd of followers and hangers-on. Somehow, even the school uniform looked different on her, hanging gracefully off her bony shoulders as if she was a model. And she had a loud, sarcastic voice and a fearsome reputation for putting people down. Even the sixth form boys were in awe of her.

Today, however, Carly was not wearing school uniform. She had on a pair of black leggings and purple DM's. She was wearing a green crushed velvet jacket and a big floppy hat. Strings of beads hung down almost to her waist and her fingernails were painted deep purple.

'Ugh!' Melissa pulled a face, 'What does she think she looks like? My mum would have kittens if I went around dressed like that.'

'So would mine,' Melanie agreed fervently. She watched, fascinated as Carly helped herself to some bright pink eyeshadow and applied it very professionally to her eyelids. Her mouth was covered in deep purple lipstick, to match her fingernails and her boots. Suddenly aware that she had acquired an audience, Carly straightened up and turned round.

'Oh look,' she drawled, 'it's the two little Christians. Having fun, are you?'

'Yeah, Carly,' Melissa shot straight back, 'we're having a great time. How about you?'

Carly glanced at herself in the full-length mirror on the pillar behind Melissa's head, and smiled complacently.

'I'm just fine,' she purred. Then, fumbling in the

35

tiny bag she wore slung around her thin body, she produced a packet of cigarettes. 'Fag?'

'No thanks — we don't smoke,' Melissa told her coldly.

'No, you don't, do you? Silly me, I forgot.'

Carly stuck a cigarette into her purple-coloured mouth and lit the end with a tiny gold lighter. Melanie stared, hypnotised as she inhaled deeply and blew a stream of smoke out of her nostrils.

The assistant behind the counter glared at them and pointed to a clearly displayed sign that read 'No Smoking'.

'Let's get out of here,' Carly said, 'I need some fresh air.' The two girls followed her, not quite sure why they were doing so.

Outside in the street, Carly leant back against the shop window and surveyed the passing shoppers. She's obviously waiting for some good-looking boy to go by, Melissa thought to herself.

'So,' Carly remarked languidly, taking another big drag on her cigarette, 'doing anything exciting tonight?'

'No,' Melanie said.

'Thought not. Strikes me that you never do anything really exciting, do you?' Carly sneered, staring at them with her lip curled scornfully. 'I mean, you never do anything at all, do you?'

'Well, actually,' Melissa said, stung into action by her sarcastic attitude, 'I'm going out somewhere.'

Rats, she thought, that's blown it. Why did I have to open my big mouth!

Carly raised her black pencilled eyebrows. 'Yeah?' she replied, incredulously. 'Where to? A prayer meeting?'

'No,' Melissa plunged on recklessly, 'I'm going out

with Justin Adams on a date, if you really want to know.'

Carly's eyes widened and she choked on her cigarette. She started coughing and the two girls hastily took a few steps back.

'Justin Adams asked *you* out?' she spluttered. 'You're kidding!'

'Nope,' Melissa replied.

Carly cackled like a witch. 'Eye of bat; toe of frog', Melissa thought to herself, remembering *Macbeth*.

'Well, well. Who'd have thought it,' Carly chuckled. 'Take some advice from me, kiddy, watch yourself with that Justin. He eats innocent little girls like you for breakfast.'

'What do you mean?' Melissa demanded, indignantly.

'Well, chicken,' Carly said, flicking her hair over her bony shoulders, 'it's not for me to say. But I'd wear a lock on my knickers, if I were you! Oh look, there's Andy and Simon. Bye.' And with a careless wave, she was gone.

'What a witch!' Melissa exclaimed watching her go. 'She's only jealous 'cos nobody fancies her, that's all.' She heard Melanie drawing her breath in sharply and turned round. 'Sorry, Lanie, excuse the language, but she really gets to me!'

'It's not *that*,' Melanie gasped, staring at Melissa round-eyed with horror. 'You never told me that you were going out with Justin Adams!'

'Didn't I?' Melissa said, casually. 'Are you quite sure? Sorry, must have completely slipped my mind. Why, you don't have a problem with that, do you?'

'Yes I do,' Melanie told her bluntly. 'You simply can't go out with him!'

'Why not?'

'Because he's not a Christian and people who go out with non-Christians always end up losing their faith.'

'Yeah? How's that?'

'Well, because they start putting the other person before God, don't they?' Melanie declared emphatically. 'Besides, it says in the Bible . . .'

'No it doesn't!' Melissa interrupted quickly. 'I just knew you'd come up with that one so I checked it out for myself and *nowhere* in the Bible does it say that you can't go out with non-Christians. OK, you shouldn't get married to them, but I'm not planning on marrying Justin Adams, am I? We're just spending some time together, as friends. No law against that, is there?'

'But Melissa,' Melanie's eyes were huge behind her glasses, 'you know it's wrong, I can tell you do. Anyway, what on earth would your mum say?'

'My mum is still in hospital,' Melissa replied, defiantly, 'so she isn't going to find out. And my dad never notices what's going on, he's always so preoccupied with his job. Anyway,' she snapped, 'it's not really any of their business. Nor is it any of yours. It's my life and I'll go out with whoever I want. So rack off!'

She glared at poor Melanie, daring her to say anything else. Trust her to try and spoil things for me, she thought. Trust her to go dragging the Bible into it!

'But Justin Adams. . .,' Melanie was obviously not going to give up easily on this one, 'he's been out with ever so many girls. He's got a really terrible reputation.'

'So he's experienced,' Melissa replied, airily dismissive. 'Great. Doesn't worry me. I've read the pamphlets. I've seen the film. I know what I'm doing. I can handle myself, no problem.'

She turned and started walking away from Melanie down the street.

'Want to come back for a Coke?' she called carelessly over her shoulder.

'No,' Melanie answered stubbornly.

'Suit yourself. Bye then. See you Monday.'

She hurried down the road, feeling Melanie's eyes boring holes in her back. Stupid girl! She didn't understand anything. She was just trying to spoil things. Well, Melissa wasn't going to let her. Tonight was special. It was going to be the most perfect evening ever. She glanced at her watch – four-thirty. Time to go home, wash her hair and get ready for her dream date with Justin.

'Yeah . . . it was *totally* brilliant,' Melissa enthused.

She and Melanie were dawdling over their lunch in the canteen. It was Monday, so Melissa had had twenty four hours to get her act together and work out exactly what she was going to say and now she was in full flow.

'I had a *great* time. I mean, Justin's such an interesting person to be with. So much to talk about. Yeah . . . I definitely prefer older guys, they're so much more sophisticated.'

Melanie regarded her friend stony-faced. Actually, she was barely speaking to Melissa and she was thinking secretly that this all sounded a bit over the top, even for her.

'So I suppose you're seeing him again?' she asked coldly.

'Er . . . possibly,' Melissa replied vaguely. 'Well, you know how it is – pressure of work, that sort of thing. I told him I didn't want any commitments. Not at

39

this stage, anyway. Let's just take it day by day, I said.'

'Maybe you could invite him to the Christian Union after half-term?' Melanie was trying very hard to find some justification for this totally improbable relationship. After all, she reasoned, Melissa was her friend, and one should stick by a friend. Even if the friend, in Melanie's opinion, was on the brink of committing spiritual suicide.

Melissa swallowed. 'Umm . . . well . . . it's certainly a thought,' she fluffed.

Just then, Melissa saw Carly Salter and two of her supporters club making their way over to her table, and to make matters worse, Carly was grinning wickedly. Cripes, she thought, her heart sinking, now I'm for it.

Carly slapped her tray down onto the table and slid into the chair opposite Melissa.

'So,' she purred delightedly, 'rumour has it that you bombed out on your date with Justin.' Her two cronies sniggered to each other as they sat down.

'Dunno what you're talking about,' Melissa replied, casually.

'Oh, *come* on!' Carly ripped the top off a yoghurt and stirred the contents round and round with her plastic spoon. She only needs a cauldron and a black hat to complete the picture, Melissa thought.

'*I* heard on the grapevine, that you couldn't handle it,' Carly continued, spooning bright pink yoghurt into her mouth. '*I* heard that you jumped out of his car and vanished into the night. Isn't it true then?'

'Erm. . .,' Melissa floundered.

'No, it's not!' Melanie broke in, loyally. 'She had a wonderful time and she and Justin got on like a house on fire.'

Melissa groaned inwardly. This was all getting worse

every second. Why hadn't she kept her big mouth shut!

'*She* told you that?' Carly said, indicating Melissa and opening her eyes wide in astonishment. Everybody turned to look at her and Melissa went bright red and stared down at her plate.

'Hmm. Well maybe you should re-check,' Carly said. 'Anyway, as far as I'm concerned, it's not important. What I wanted to tell you was that I just found out the reason Justin asked you out in the first place. It appears that he had a bet on with some of his mates that he could get off with one of you Christian girls, and the story is that he's well out of pocket at the moment. Apparently he and his mates reckoned that you'd be easy as you're all so desperate that you'd get the hots for anyone. Well, that's the story going round.'

'The hots?' Melanie squeaked. 'What do you mean "the hots"?'

'Isn't she amazing?' Carly drawled to her admiring fan club, who were staring at Melanie incredulously. 'Straight out of Sunday School!'

She finished her yoghurt, stuck the spoon into the empty carton and stood up. 'Must go. Things to see to. Anyway, I'd keep a pretty low profile for a week or so, if I were you. Just until Justin's mates have let him off the hook.'

Then, surprisingly, she grinned at Melissa. 'Though if you want my opinion, it's high time something like this happened to him. He and his little crowd think they're God's gift to women, so basically, you did us all a favour there, kid. Whether you meant to, or not.'

She picked up her tray and sauntered off, her cronies following behind her, laughing, leaving Melissa sitting there in an acute state of shock, staring open-mouthed after them.

A bet? Justin had a *bet*? There she was thinking that he really fancied her and all the time, he was trying to prove something to his mates, and using her to do it. She felt as flat as a burst balloon. She had honestly believed that Justin liked her but he'd just been playing some game with her. All at once, she felt so *ashamed*. She wanted to dig a hole and bury herself in it for the rest of her life!

'So what really did happen?' Melanie asked, regarding her curiously.

Melissa sighed. If only she'd kept quiet. Or told the truth in the first place. Or, best of all, listened to Melanie and her own conscience and turned Justin down flat.

'It was awful, Lanie,' she blurted out, feeling almost near to tears, 'really awful. For a start, he picked me up in this flash car he'd borrowed off his parents – he didn't even come to the door, just waited outside, and hooted for me to come out.'

'How rude!'

'Quite. Then, he drove really fast – I'm sure he went through a red light and all the time he kept on looking in the mirror and flicking his hair back. He never said anything about how nice I looked. And I did,' she added, defiantly.

'How dreadful.'

'Oh, it gets worse. So then, we went to the Galleria cinema and they were showing one of those really horrible films – you know, all full of swearing and people having sex every two seconds. I'm sure we shouldn't have been allowed in. It was disgusting. I didn't know where to look. And then, half way through, he started *groping* me.'

'He *what*?'

'You know, the hand across the back of the seat

routine. Except it didn't stop there. Honestly, it was like sitting next to an octopus. And he kept *breathing* at me. I think he thought it would turn me on or something. Anyway, when the film finished, he drove me home the longest way possible and then suddenly, he stopped the car and said it had run out of petrol.'

'And?'

'Well, I was really fed up by this time, so I told him that I'd rather get out and walk the rest of the way back. And the next minute he was all over me. Kissing me and stuff. It felt like being attacked by a maniac slug. It was utterly gross! So I pushed him off and got out of the car and ran all the way home. And that's the honest truth.'

She stared miserably at Melanie who by now was totally goggle-eyed. 'Go on, say it. "I told you so".'

Melanie shook her head. 'No need. is there? Anyway, I wouldn't say it in the first place – you're my friend.' She smiled. 'But I'm glad you're not seeing him again. I could never understand what everyone sees in him. I've always thought he was a first-class creep.'

Melissa felt the ghost of a smile returning to her face. Good old Melanie, she thought to herself. Loyal to the bitter end. Where would she be without her!

Then suddenly, a horrible thought struck her. 'What if everybody finds out?' she wailed. 'I'll never be able to face them. I'll have to change schools. I'll have to leave the country!'

'Don't worry,' Melanie cut in reassuringly, 'it probably won't happen. Like Carly said, Justin's pride has been hurt and he's a bit out of pocket, that's all. I don't think he'd really want everybody to know that you didn't fall for him, would he? After all, that'd make him look a complete fool. So I think he'll try hard to kill the story. And if I were you, I'd do the same. And I'd avoid Justin Adams like the plague from now on. Horrid boy! At least he's found out that we're not a pushover. What a nerve!' Melanie's cheeks had gone quite pink in her indignation.

'No, we're certainly not,' Melissa echoed fervently.

But you so nearly were, she thought ruefully. Anyway, she reminded herself, only a few more days until half-term and, with a bit of luck everyone will have forgotten all about it by the time we go back.

~ 5 ~

Melissa had made plans for a quiet half-term. Nothing too taxing, nothing too energetic and definitely nothing embarrassing. A little studying, she had decided, mixed with some window shopping and some light housework, that sort of thing. Well, rather a lot of studying, actually. She had not done spectacularly well in her course work so far this term, and a few not very subtle hints had been dropped by several teachers that she needed to pull her socks up and get down to some serious work in the not too distant future.

Or, as Mrs Hobson tersely put it, 'Hit the books or hit the road!'

Yes, a nice, peaceful week would just suit her fine. It would help her to forget the painful memory of her disastrous date with Justin. And it looked as if she was to get what she wanted.

Alice had gone to stay with one of her friends until Thursday, Dad was heading up a course in Plymouth, and Alex was 'around' but as usual, not too much.

Most of her school friends had gone away – skiing or staying with grandparents, and those that were left had also drawn up elaborate plans for the amazing amounts of studying that they all intended to do. Even Melanie was away for the week. She, her family and the rest of her church had gone off to some holiday camp in Wales for King's Week, the annual get-together for their fellowship.

It was an event that Melissa had come to dread because Melanie always returned from King's Week totally over the top and went around witnessing furiously to everyone she met. Usually, Melissa spent the first week back at school de-programming her and trying to steer her away from trouble. Melanie always invited Melissa to come to King's Week with her, but Melissa never went. Somehow, she didn't fancy a week going to seminars and singing choruses – even though Melanie always assured her that the teenagers had a great time, with special events laid on for them, and they were allowed to stay up all hours.

Over the years of their friendship, Melissa had come to the regrettable conclusion that Melanie was a 'better' Christian than she was. Even her house reflected it, Melissa thought to herself.

The Pearson's house was impeccably neat and tidy, with plain dark carpets and plain dark wood furniture and wall to wall books on every aspect of Christianity in the living room. The Pearsons also went in for texts – they had one in the kitchen which went on about Christ being the Unseen listener to every conversation and the Unseen watcher of everything that went on. Once, Melissa recollected, when she was sleeping over, she had to get up in the night to go to the toilet, and she had found her eyes drifting round the bathroom, wondering whether God was actually watching her on the loo, which made her feel quite uncomfortable. So she had declined the offer of King's Week, saying, 'Maybe next year.'

It was what she always said.

Melissa spent most of Monday morning drawing up a timetable for the week. It looked very professional. Each subject had its own morning or afternoon slot. Even the great Anne Frank could not have done better, she thought, pinning the timetable triumphantly to her memo board.

However she found that as the week went on, it was all very well intending to work, but quite another thing actually getting down to do any. Somehow, there were always so many distractions. For instance, Caron phoned on Tuesday morning (English literature and French) to say that her mum had got a new catalogue and there was a ten per cent discount on all summer clothes and would she like to pop round and have a sneak preview in case there was anything that she wanted to order. That took care of the morning and in the afternoon, Melissa placed a rather large order, which she knew she couldn't really afford, but hoped to pay for by scrounging off Dad when he was in a good mood, which meant she simply had to go through her wardrobe and sort out all her summer stuff.

Then, on Wednesday morning, (Biology and Chemistry) feeling very virtuous, she took a big bag of cast-offs down to Oxfam, where she just happened to run into some friends and spent the rest of the day hanging around, gossiping, listening to tapes and watching boys at the Hard Rock Record Store and doing nothing in particular.

It was rather pleasant, Melissa decided, being able

to go where she wanted, not having to rush back to check on supper. It was certainly nice not being at school, where she had spent the last few days constantly looking over her shoulder in case she should bump into Justin or any of his mates. Her confidence had taken a bit of a battering, but by the end of the week, Melissa felt she had bounced back. None of her friends had mentioned the Justin affair, so it looked like she had managed to come out of it still smelling of roses. And to top it all, she was still just about managing to run the house and do some of her school work at the same time. She had even managed to find time to make a big chocolate cake to welcome Alice home on Thursday, (History and Maths).

Yes, it was good to be in control, Melissa decided. The problems of the last week or two were safely behind her now. They had finished nearly all the shepherd's pie and apple crumble in the freezer and anyway, Mum was coming home in two weeks' time. Life was going to be a breeze.

Alice was dropped off just before tea on Thursday afternoon. She rushed in and hugged Melissa ecstatically.

'I missed you!' she yelled.

Melissa returned the hug. She hadn't really missed Alice, as she had been too busy, but it was still good to have her back. Alice had been pretty OK since Mum went into hospital, she thought. At least she had *tried* to be helpful, unlike some members of the family, who seemed to think that she was only there to wait on them hand and foot.

Alice went upstairs to sort out her stuff. There was silence for five minutes. Then, suddenly, Melissa heard a scream followed by loud sobbing and Alice's voice wailed down, 'Mel! Mel, something dreadful's happened!'

Melissa pounded upstairs. Alice was bending over her cage of gerbils, holding something in her cupped hands.

'Oh no, tell me I'm not seeing this, somebody,' Melissa groaned. 'The gerbils! I forgot all about them!'

Alice raised her tear-stained face. Her shoulders were shaking with sobs and great fat tears were pouring down her cheeks. 'They're both dead! Look, Mel, they haven't had any food for days.' She cradled the two pathetic little bundles in her hands.

Melissa felt a great wave of pity and anger rising up inside her. She didn't believe it! How could she possibly have gone and forgotten Alice's gerbils? And just when she thought she had everything under control. If only she hadn't been so busy rushing around.

'So why didn't *you* feed them before you went?' she snarled.

'Mum always reminded me,' Alice hiccupped.

And you were so busy looking at clothes and enjoying yourself with your friends that you didn't remember either, Melissa's conscience reminded her. It wasn't Alice's fault, she told herself. It wasn't her fault either. It was just that she simply couldn't think of everything all at the same time. Melissa struggled to contain her feelings. Mum, she groaned inwardly, please come home, we need you!

She put a comforting arm round Alice's shoulders. 'I'm sorry, Beastly,' she said gently, giving her sister the old, familiar pet name. 'I'm really, really sorry. Look, it's not the end of the world, honestly. We'll get you some more gerbils at the weekend. And I've got a really pretty gift box in my room. We can put Snowy and Ginger in it and give them a proper funeral in the garden after tea.'

Alice sniffed and dragged her grubby sleeve across her streaming eyes. 'Have they gone to heaven, now?' she asked pathetically.

Melissa frowned. She was not very well up on Small Rodent Theology. How on earth did Mum handle this sort of stuff? 'Umm . . . I'm sure God is looking after them somewhere,' she replied vaguely.

She took the two lifeless little animals from Alice and laid them carefully on the floor of the cage.

'Tea,' she said firmly. 'Come on.'

When Alex breezed in later that afternoon, he found them both sitting gloomily at the kitchen table.

'What's up?' he inquired.

'Don't ask,' Melissa sighed, shaking her head warningly at him.

They buried the gerbils after tea. Alex dug a hole in the back garden and Alice solemnly placed the little gift box into it, still sniffing, whilst Melissa said a short, hastily improvised prayer over the grave.

'You could have pulled the Everlasting Gerbil trick on her,' Alex remarked later, when Alice and her grief had at last been coaxed to bed.

'The what?' Melissa asked with a puzzled frown.

'You know. Remember Hawley Road Primary School?'

'Not unless I absolutely have to.'

'Yeah well, we used to have these two gerbils, called Salt and Pepper, didn't we?'

'I remember them – in Mrs Jones' class.'

'Exactly. They were still there when you went to that school – how many years after me was that?'

'Must've been three or four.'

50

'And how long do the little perishers live for?'

'A couple of years. Oh, I *see*,' Melissa exclaimed, light finally beginning to dawn, 'You mean they used to replace the gerbils without any of the kids realising it!'

'Got it in one. You didn't do death properly until the Juniors, did you? Ancient Egyptians, I think it came in there. So, whenever one of the gerbils passed on to the great gerbil run in the sky, one of the staff nipped out to Bettapets and bought a replacement. Neat, eh? I mean, one gerbil looks identical to another. They don't go in for any great distinguishing features, like glasses or wooden legs, so it worked a treat. They must've kept whole generations of infants blissfully happy that way.'

Melissa looked thoughtful, 'You know, you're absolutely right. Those gerbils were still there when Alice started. She used to bring them home for the weekend. That's how all this pet business started. Once she'd gone up to the Juniors, she developed Gerbil Withdrawal Syndrome, so Mum bought her Snowy and Ginger.'

'Now alas, Snowy and Ginger, RIP,' Alex said, ruefully. 'Pity you didn't think to replace them.'

Melissa pulled a face. 'I would have done it, if only I'd gone into her room earlier,' she said.

'Ah well,' Alex said, 'there you go. Easy to be wise after the event isn't it? Mind you,' he added maddeningly, 'if you'd gone into her room earlier, they'd still be alive and squeaking now, wouldn't they?'

Melissa could still hear her sister sobbing to herself until late in the night, and she knew she would have to replace the gerbils as soon as possible, and unless Alex chipped in, out of her own money, which meant saying goodbye to one of the T-shirts she had picked out for herself from Caron's mum's catalogue. Why did something always have to go wrong just when she was getting her life together? It was a strange thing, but the more she thought about it, the more she was beginning to wonder whether she was really in control after all!

On Friday morning, Melissa actually managed to study until lunch. More surprising still, Alex actually volunteered to do the washing, aided by Alice, who was still in mourning for her gerbils. It was only the promise that they would all go into town on Saturday and choose some more from the pet shop, that was keeping her from breaking down all over again.

In the afternoon, Melissa decided to go for a walk, on her own. She needed to get out of the house, away from Alice's sorrowful face, which kept bringing her out in a severe attack of guilt whenever she looked at her. She walked briskly up Ox Lane and decided to cut through the alleyway to Westfield Road. It was a mild spring day and there were loads of flowers out in the front gardens. She walked on, remembering the number of times she had gone this way before, usually with Steve on their way back from church. It gave her a strange, nostalgic feeling, thinking about the past. Things had seemed far easier in those days.

She turned into Westfield Road. The old bus shelter was still there, half way down the hill. She was surprised to see it still in one piece, as the bus had long since ceased to run. She decided to stroll down and see if the seat was still there too and as she got nearer she saw that not only was the seat still there but there was somebody actually sitting inside the shelter. It looked like . . . was it? . . . yeah, she knew that green baseball cap. It was Steve. That's a coincidence, Melissa thought to herself, just as I was thinking about him. Then, she remembered their last bruising encounter at school and stopped. Did she really want a repeat performance? Maybe it would be better just to turn round and go back the way she had come.

She stood for a moment, hovering uncertainly between the two choices. Then abruptly, she made up her mind. She would stroll casually by and say hello. After all, she reasoned, Steve was on his own this time. Maybe he would be different without his creepy mates. She walked down the hill until she drew level with the shelter.

Steve was sitting hunched in a corner, staring down at his shoes. He did not move or look up as Melissa approached him. In fact, he didn't even seem to notice that somebody had come up to him at all.

'Hi Steve,' Melissa said briskly, in a very casual take-it-or-leave-it voice.

Steve looked up at her. For a moment, he seemed not to recognise who she was. Then, he gave her a strange, crooked smile.

'Well, it's ol' Melly,' he said. 'Smelly ol' Melly!' He seemed to find this very funny, and repeated it several times, chuckling weirdly to himself.

Melissa stared down at him. There was something very wrong with him, she thought. Steve's voice was all slurred, and his face looked kind of blurry round the edges. He also seemed to be having some difficulty in focusing his eyes upon her and his skin was a peculiar colour, like he was just about to be sick.

'What's the matter with you?' Melissa asked him. 'Aren't you feeling well or what?'

Steve tried to stand up, but after a few attempts, he gave up the unequal struggle and slumped back down into his corner.

'S'nothing wrong with me,' he declared. 'Pig off!'

'Steve,' Melissa said sternly, 'have you been drinking?'

'Nah,' Steve drawled, finally managing to haul himself up onto his feet. 'Don't drink. Notatall.'

'Then what on earth have you been doing?'

Steve stared muzzily at her, swaying gently from side to side. A little rivulet of spit ran down his chin. He tried to wipe it away with his sleeve but couldn't quite manage to get his arm up to his face.

'You go away,' he told Melissa fiercely. 'It's none of your business. I don't wanna see you. Stuff you. And stuff your pigging God too. I got better things to do now. Go on, you heard me, didn't you? Go away.'

Melissa opened her mouth to say something equally scathing in reply, but she couldn't think of anything to say. If only Melanie were here, she thought desperately, she'd know how to handle this.

She was very shocked by Steve's condition. She had never seen anybody in such a mess before. Was he drunk? But he said he hadn't been drinking and there were no empty cans or bottles on the ground. Only a plastic Sainsbury's carrier bag which looked to be empty. Automatically, Melissa bent down to pick it up and put it in the bin, but before she could, Steve unexpectedly leaned towards her and snatched the bag out of her hand.

'That's mine!' he shouted, holding the bag against his body. He glared at Melissa, his eyes focusing and unfocusing and his mouth hanging slightly open.

All at once, Melissa began to feel scared. What was wrong with him? Should she try to get some help, or what?

Then, suddenly, Steve's mood seemed to change, and he calmed down. He grinned stupidly at her.

'Gotta go now, Smelly,' he announced letting go of the shelter and swaying to and fro in the entrance, 'see ya 'round.'

He lurched out of the shelter and began to walk with unsteady footsteps up the hill towards the town centre. Melissa watched him go, wishing that she had said or done more to help. She felt totally useless. If only she knew what was the matter with Steve.

Just as he turned the corner, she noticed that he had dropped the plastic bag. She ran after him and picked it up. To her surprise, there was something in it after all. She opened up the bag and peered in. And then, Melissa realised what was wrong with Steve, and knew with a cold sinking feeling in her heart that he was in very serious trouble indeed.

Oh God, she thought desperately, how on earth am I supposed to handle this?

~ 6 ~

'Honestly, Melissa,' Melanie said, custard dropping unnoticed from her spoon, 'you really should have come. It was fantastic. Absolutely brill. All the church worshipping together. I mean, that's what it's really about, isn't it? Praising God and sharing. Being one in the Spirit.'

Melissa closed her eyes and tried to pretend she was somewhere else. Preferably on another planet. It was happening all over again. Just like last year and the year before. Melanie holding forth at full volume and everyone else avoiding them like the plague. She opened her eyes wearily and stared out over Melanie's left shoulder, nodding at regular intervals but not really listening to a word she was saying. She was to regret this.

'So don't you think it's a brill idea?' Melanie suddenly asked, leaning forwards, her eyes sparkling fanatically behind her glasses.

'Er. . .,' Melissa floundered helplessly. What on earth had Melanie been talking about? Her mind backtracked furiously. It threw up Geography test. Followed by Cleaning the house before Mum came home on Saturday and Must find out the name of that good-looking boy on the next table. No, she had to admit to herself that she honestly hadn't heard a single word for the last five minutes.

'Umm . . . yeah . . . great,' she said, hoping that she had selected the correct answer.

'You agree then?'

'Agree about what?'

'Chuck Faithful.'

'Who?'

Melanie sighed deeply and gave Melissa a reproach-ful look.

'The American evangelist I was just telling you about. The one who did the Youth Programme at King's Week. Honestly, Melissa were you listening or what?'

'Yeah, of course I was listening,' Melissa lied. 'It's just that I must have got temporarily distracted or something. So tell me again about this Chuck whats-isname.'

'Chuck Faithful,' Melanie corrected her. 'He's really good. We all liked him. Very down to earth and relevant. So I thought, as he's coming to do a week's training programme at my church, we could ask him to do the CU.'

'Our CU?'

'Yes.'

'Here?'

'Yes.'

'But he wouldn't be interested, would he?'

'Oh yes he would. He's staying at our house and I asked him last night. He says he'd love to do it.' Melanie got up. 'Great. I'm so glad you think it's a good idea too. I'll go and tell the committee. I thought we could use it to do some real outreach, for a change. See you...'

'Er... Lanie,' Melissa began, 'before you go, I wanted to talk to you about Steve Hayes – I think he might be...' But she was talking to herself. Melanie was already over the other side of the canteen, bending the ear of the CU president.

Melissa stared down at her empty plate and groaned inwardly. Outreach. She hated that word. Over the past few years she had come to dread Melanie's attempts to do outreach. Not that she was against outreach in principle. After all, it was scriptural, wasn't it? It was just that somehow, outreach always seemed to involve her getting into embarrassing situations and being laughed at. She knew that didn't bother Melanie at all, but it bothered her.

'You have to be prepared to stand up and be counted,' Melanie told her once, to which Melissa had replied that she definitely preferred keeping her head down and being overlooked.

It was going to be a difficult few weeks, that was for sure. And who on earth was this Chuck Faithful? What a name! Could anybody *really* be called that? Whoever he was, Melissa thought, let's face it, he was wasting his time coming to their CU.

The CU was not exactly one of the most universally popular lunch time activities. There were so many other things happening on Wednesday that going to the CU never got to the top of everybody's list of favourite things to do. Week by week, it successfully failed to pull in the crowds. Maybe this also had something to do with its location – H3 was a glorified cupboard on the second floor of the science block. Its walls were painted pale grey, except for the areas where the paint was peeling off and there was only really room for ten people to sit in relative comfort. There was no heating, so in winter, everybody had to wear their coats and in summer, the one tiny window had to be kept wide open otherwise people complained of feeling faint from lack of oxygen. This window looked out onto the back of the staff car park and provided a golden opportunity for Darren and his mates to disrupt the meetings by standing underneath and singing loudly throughout the choruses or shouting obscenities during the prayer times. Numbers fluctuated, depending upon what else was on, or the time of year, or who had exams looming and usually, only the very dedicated few went regularly. Melanie was one of the very dedicated few, of course. Melissa meant to go along every week, as she had promised herself she would, but hadn't quite managed to put in a complete run of appearances yet. She had almost convinced herself that *meaning* to go was practically the same thing as actually being there, and that anyway, somebody had to spend time with all the non-Christian girls in the class, otherwise how would they get saved? But if she was really honest with herself, the truth was that anything was better than being packed like sardines into that drab, stuffy little room, trying to sing 'Majesty' to a background of rude noises.

Outreach. It was a total waste of time in this school, Melissa decided. And after all, there was barely enough room for the present members of the CU. If it got any bigger, they would have to take it in turns breathing!

'B4?' exclaimed Melissa. 'How on earth did you manage to get B4? That's reserved for special meetings.'

Melanie smiled smugly. She had been smiling smugly for several days now, and it was beginning to get on Melissa's nerves. Just because Chuck Faithful was staying with her parents, Melanie had been co-opted onto the CU committee and she was enjoying her new role in a way that really got up Melissa's nose. All she wanted to do was talk endlessly about Chuck's visit and the plans that were being made. She had no time to spare to listen to Melissa and Melissa just wasn't used to being pushed aside. Right now, she was finding it very hard to be nice to Melanie.

'Well, we're expecting loads of kids to come,' Melanie replied. 'Haven't you seen the posters?' She waved an arm in the direction of the double doors at the end of the corridor. Melissa stared in the direction of the arm and noticed a large, fluorescent yellow poster. It definitely hadn't been there at break time.

'COME AND MEET THE FAMOUS AMERICAN FOOTBALL STAR – CHUCK FAITHFUL, WEDNESDAY AT 12:15, ROOM B4,' it read in large black capital letters.

'Famous *football* star?' Melissa queried. 'You didn't say anything about that before.'

'Didn't I?' Melanie replied vaguely. 'Are you sure?'

'Quite sure,' Melissa countered. 'So what team does he play for then?'

'The Hicksville Hotsox,' Melanie told her.

'*Who?*'

'That's his home team in Arizona. And he doesn't actually play for them now – but he used to when he was younger.'

'Well, it's hardly the Chicago Bears, is it?' said Melissa, very sarcastically. 'I bet nobody's ever heard of them. And another thing. . .' she peered at the poster again, 'it doesn't say anything about the CU on that poster.'

'Yes it does,' Melanie countered. 'Bottom left-hand corner.'

Melissa walked up to the poster and looked. There, in letters so small that you needed a magnifying-glass to see them clearly, were written the words, 'a CU presentation'.

'Oh yeah, so it does,' she said sarcastically. 'Not exactly *obvious* though, is it? I mean, I could have missed it, if you hadn't told me. And another thing,' Melissa continued, getting into her stride, 'what's all this about a sports talk? I thought he was coming to do outreach.'

'Ah yes, well, I wondered when you'd notice that,' Melanie replied brightly. 'It's called creative advertising. It's Matthew's idea, really. You have to find the right angle – one that will appeal to the maximum amount of people, and make the most of it – in this case, it's sport.'

'But isn't it a bit dishonest?' Melissa pursued. 'I mean, you're supposed to be Christians for goodness sake. I think it's being a bit economical with the truth.'

'No, it's not at all dishonest,' Melanie replied indignantly. 'Actually, it's very scriptural. It says in the Bible that you should be prepared to use every method available to get people interested in Christianity and everyone knows that good advertising brings results. Anyway, how often have you bought something which looked great on the TV and turned out to be a dead loss? So, people may be coming to hear a sports talk, but they'll really be getting something far better. Sort of reverse-advertising, if you like. You get more than you thought you were getting, rather than less.'

'And I suppose Matthew told you that, too?' Melissa remarked acidly.

Matthew Devine was the CU president. He was in the upper sixth. He was tall and fairly good-looking if you went for the serious, academic type. Matthew Devine always carried a small Bible around with him wherever he went. Sometimes he even got it out and read it in the Common Room. Matthew went to Melanie's church, and Melissa often wondered why they hadn't got it together yet. They seemed ideally suited to each other. She could picture them strolling hand in hand through the park, discussing theology and swapping their favourite verses.

'Yes he did, actually,' Melanie said, 'and I think he's quite right, if you want to know. So, are you coming along to support us, or what?'

'Yeah,' Melissa sighed deeply, 'OK, I'll come.'

She turned and walked away. If only Melanie was not quite so busy putting up posters and attending planning meetings. She really needed to talk to somebody about Steve. She was worried about him. Very worried. There was definitely something wrong with him — she suspected that there had been for quite some time, and now, after what she had seen over half-term, she knew for sure that it was serious and that he needed help. Whatever was driving him, it went far deeper than his rudeness to her and his refusal to come near the church. Those were only the outward symptoms. Something pretty drastic had happened to Steve and it had turned him into a new and rather dangerous person.

Melissa felt powerless and, if she was completely honest with herself, a bit scared too. She didn't know what to do for the best. She just wasn't sure how to reach Steve any more. It seemed such a long time since those far off days when they had been friends. Nowadays, they couldn't seem to communicate at all

– they didn't even seem to speak the same language any more. She needed to confide in Melanie – but whenever she broached the subject, all Melanie would say was, 'Yeah, right. Why not invite him along to the meeting?'

Somehow, Melissa felt that going to the CU was the very last thing that Steve wanted to do right now, and if she asked him, which she had no intention of doing of course, it would only make him more hostile and drive him even further away.

It was strange, she thought, the way that Steve kept straying into her mind. After all, it was not as if she even liked him. Not any more. He had been too rude and he had humiliated her in front of all her mates. And it was quite plain that he didn't like her. So why did he keep returning to haunt her at all the most inappropriate moments? Here she was, for instance, right in the middle of her homework, (a half-hour English assignment that was actually taking nearly two hours – they always did) when she suddenly realised that her mind was no longer on her work. She was trying to remember when she had last seen Steve at school. Not for a couple of days, she was sure. So where was he then? Sick? Perhaps. Maybe bunking off school. Yeah, probably. Hanging out with his mates somewhere sniffing glue. Maybe even worse.

A sudden vision of Steve rose in front of her eyes – his fair hair all spiky with gel, blue eyes scowling at her, his green baseball cap, the one he called his 'lucky hat' worn back to front, as usual. She put down her pen and stared out of the window. Frog it! She didn't *want* to think about him, but she couldn't help herself. It was as if somebody kept planting him into her brain. Maybe it was God. Melissa groaned. Obviously she needed to put God straight about a few things.

She closed her eyes. 'Look God,' she reasoned, 'forget it. OK? I've got better things to think about. And anyway, I'm not the right person to talk to Steve. He hates me. He wouldn't listen. Find somebody else.'

Melissa opened her eyes. Maybe she had resolved to do something about Steve back in the New Year, but she hadn't realised just what that 'something' was going to involve. And now she did, she wanted out. Quite definitely out.

And there was another thing, Melissa thought, continuing to stare angrily out of the window, where was her so-called best friend when she needed her? Too busy to listen. Too preoccupied with her own affairs to care. It was ironic, wasn't it? That when she didn't want her advice, Melanie was right there, interfering with her bits from the Bible, but now, when Melissa had a real crisis upon her hands, she couldn't even spare her the time of day. Locked into the CU scam, that's where she was. For Melissa believed that it was a scam, however much Matthew tried to justify it. She wasn't stupid enough to swallow all that 'using every method available' line for one second. Mind you, she thought, with a quick grin, they may well pull in the crowds, but how on earth were they going to keep them once the kids realised that they had been conned. There would be a mass stampede for the door and the whole fiasco would end in egg on faces all round. They were really going to look stupid. All that time and effort wasted. It will jolly well serve Melanie right for neglecting me, she thought self-righteously, as she dragged her mind kicking and screaming back to her English homework.

On Saturday morning, Melissa, Alice and Alex cleaned the whole house from top to bottom. Melissa had spent days drumming it into both of them that the house had to be totally spotless for Mum's return or else the repercussions would be too terrible to contemplate. Alice was so overcome by this threat that she actually took a large duster to bed with her, so that she would be ready to start as soon as she woke up. Melissa had not been sure how Alex would react, so was totally surprised when not only did he report in next morning bright and early, but also promised that Tasha, his latest girlfriend would come over and help too.

Tasha was a complete revelation! She was tiny, with a thick dark brown fringe and huge blue eyes that peered out from underneath, giving her face the appearance of a lovesick spaniel. She wore denim dungarees which made her look about eight years old. Even Alice had stopped wearing dungarees by now. Tasha had a breathy little voice and was studying Home Economics, so that, she told Melissa, she would know how to cook and look after a house when she got married. Getting married appeared to be Tasha's main aim in life and by mid-morning, Melissa, who had always dreamed of a brilliant career for herself (somehow fitting a husband and a home around it) was beginning to feel decidedly fed up with being told that, 'a woman's first duty is to look after her man.'

Poor Alice, who had almost developed a flat head from the number of times Tasha had patted it, was looking slightly sick. Melissa didn't have the heart to tell Tasha, who kept shooting lovesick glances in Alex's direction, that she was wasting her breath going on about getting married, because he was plugged into his Walkman, and couldn't hear a word she was saying.

And on Saturday, at long last, Mum came home from the hospital.

~ 7 ~

'AAYY – MEN!!' The man's voice suddenly soared above the chatter.

Everybody instantly stopped talking and turned round to face the front of the room. A tall grey-bearded figure in blue jeans and a white T-shirt bearing the slogan – Only One Way Up – was standing there, smiling unconcernedly round. He had long grey hair, which he wore in a ponytail and at his feet was a very battered black guitar case.

Melissa blinked. So this was (presumably) the famous footballer and evangelist, Chuck Faithful. Somehow, he didn't look at all like she had imagined. She had pictured somebody in a boring black suit with one of those unsmiling, holy-looking faces. Certainly nothing like this amiable, ageing hippy guy!

She looked round the room and got another surprise. It was absolutely packed out. There were kids sharing chairs and leaning against the walls in their eagerness to see the 'famous American football star'. The room was so full, that Melissa couldn't even spot the members of the CU committee, though she decided that they were probably trying to keep their heads down, in case anybody rumbled what was really going to happen. She smiled secretly to herself. Ten minutes, she thought gleefully, I'll give him ten minutes, and then there will be a mass stampede for the door.

'Hi, y'all,' Chuck Faithful said, grinning happily as he surveyed his eagerly waiting audience. 'M' name's Chuck Faithful and I'm from the Big Country across the pond — and in case anyone of you doesn't know, that means the US of A.'

The audience smiled back, waiting for the sports talk to begin.

'Now then kids,' Chuck Faithful went on, 'I know some of you've come here wanting to learn something about sport? Well, I'm gonna tell you about a game. It's called the game of Real Life, and what I'm gonna tell ya is something I hope y'all never forget.'

There were a few puzzled glances and some doubtful murmuring. Chuck Faithful bent down, undid the guitar case, and drew out the most battered guitar Melissa had ever seen in her whole life. It was totally plastered with Christian stickers.

'And first,' Chuck Faithful announced, grinning from ear to ear as he slung the tatty leather strap around his neck, 'I'm gonna sing.' And he struck a chord on the guitar and started singing,

'*Oh, won't you drop-kick me, Jesus*
Through the goal-posts of life. . .'

He had an interesting voice, Melissa decided after the first three verses. Sort of extremely loud and gravelly. The kind of voice that could shatter windows, or stun chickens.

She looked around. Most of the audience was sitting

with their mouths open, staring in total disbelief. For a couple of verses, nobody moved a muscle, some of the kids were obviously genuinely under the impression that Jesus played for an American football team, but gradually, light began to dawn, and people realised that they had been lured into the room under false pretences. This was no sports talk. They had been conned. There was some rebellious muttering and then, as if at a given signal, the entire front row got up and headed for the exit.

I knew it! Melissa thought gleefully, turning round to watch them go. She turned back and surveyed the rest of the audience, waiting for more kids to join the exodus. But to her surprise, everybody else stayed sitting down and waited. Chuck Faithful, meanwhile, totally unthrown by the few defectors, came to the end of the song, put down his guitar, and picked up his Bible.

It wasn't so much what he said, Melissa recalled later, though he did say an awful lot, as the way he said it. Words seemed to flow out of him in a steady never-ending stream. It was the first time Melissa had ever heard an American evangelist and the effect was mesmeric. His voice rose and fell rhythmically whilst his audience just sat in complete silence and stared at him, glassy-eyed, as if in some hypnotic trance, trying to work out how on earth he managed to talk so fast and breathe at the same time. Even Melissa found herself floating away on the vast sea of words. Somewhere, outside this room, she thought dreamily to herself, life was going on as normal. Kids were gossiping together and copying each other's project notes, maybe bunking off to get some chips, but here, in this room, there was only the sound of Chuck Faithful's voice talking steadily on and on. . .

Melissa's eyes began to close. The room seemed hot and stuffy. She felt her body beginning to sway from side to side in time with what he was saying. Then, somebody's digital alarm went off shrilly and she came to with a start. She looked at her watch. Nearly time for afternoon school. She glanced up. Everybody was sitting with heads bowed. Chuck Faithful was praying. The meeting was coming to an end and she hadn't even noticed. Then Chuck said, 'Amen,' loudly and people began to get up and make for the doors, which had now been opened by some of the CU.

Melissa stood up and filed out with all the rest. At the door, she spotted Melanie, Matthew and the rest of the CU committee who had now materialised from amongst the audience and were handing out little leaflets. Mechanically, she reached out her hand and took one. *New Life in Christ – Four Easy Steps* it said on the cover.

'Mel . . . Mel!' Melanie hissed as Melissa furtively stuffed the leaflet into her pocket. 'Wasn't he brilliant?'

Melissa stared at her. Melanie's face was flushed and radiant, her eyes gleaming behind her glasses. It was obvious that she thought the meeting had been a great success. Melissa found herself cringing and hoping nobody from her class had seen her. It was so embarrassing!

'Did you see the looks on peoples' faces?' Melanie went on. 'They were totally rapt! I really think we've made an impact this time. And look at all those kids who've stayed behind for prayer!'

Melissa turned round in the doorway and looked. To her astonishment and disbelief, the front three rows were full of kids sitting and talking to Chuck Faithful and a couple of the older members of the CU. Some of the kids had their heads bowed and were quite clearly being prayed over.

Melissa made her way thoughtfully along the corridor. It was unreal. What was going on? She had mentally dismissed the whole event as a big joke and a gigantic waste of time and effort. She had even planned a few really cutting things to say to Melanie later on when all the fuss had died down. Instead, it almost looked as if the thing might be turning out to be rather a success after all.

'So why didn't you tell me sooner, Melissa?'

'I tried to, didn't I? But you were always too busy to listen.'

'Oh, yes. Right.'

'You didn't want to know, did you? "Tell me after the Chuck Faithful meeting", remember?'

'I see. I'm sorry ... but you have to admit, it *was* all worthwhile, wasn't it!'

Melissa sighed. 'Yeah,' she acknowledged grudgingly, 'I suppose so.'

For, much to her surprise (and also she suspected, to the surprise of the CU) eight kids had become Christians as a result of that meeting. So now, the CU had abandoned its programme of *Getting To Grips With Leviticus* and embarked upon a basic believers' course. And because they had grown so dramatically in numbers, they had also been given new premises – a light, airy room down the hall from the library, with windows opening out onto the school pond and nature area, so there was no more harassment from Darren and his mob. And even more amazing, one of the new Christians, a girl from Year Seven, was a quite brilliant guitarist, and had been bringing her guitar along to the meetings to help with the music. All of which meant that Melissa actually found herself beginning to look forward to Wednesday lunch times. Quite astonishing!

It was now three weeks after the meeting with Chuck Faithful, and here she was sitting on Melanie's bed. It was Saturday night and Melissa was sleeping over as it was Melanie's sixteenth birthday. Melissa always slept over at Melanie's house on her birthday. It had become a sort of ritual over the last three years. Other girls had a disco, or a pizza party, but Melanie liked to invite her best friend round for a nice supper and a sleep over.

This year, as always, they had rented a video (*Chariots of Fire*, Melanie's choice) and then after it had finished, they had decamped upstairs to Melanie's room to talk until it was time to sleep.

Melanie's parents generally gave her sensible presents for Christmas and birthday and for her sixteenth birthday, they had decided to update her study area, so that she now had a very smart pine desk with drawers on either side and a matching shelf unit above. Melanie's desk did *not* face the window, which was probably why she always managed to finish her homework on time.

Melissa had bought her a couple of good tapes — the sort that her parents called 'wall to wall noise'. She had fleetingly wondered whether she should disguise them in Christian music covers, but fortunately, Melanie's parents knew even less about pop music than hers did, and didn't throw a wobbly when Melanie unwrapped them.

'So tell me again,' Melanie said, uncurling one cramped leg from under her, 'you saw Steve in the bus shelter and he was behaving strangely?'

'Very strangely. You know, more than just being his usual rude self,' Melissa told her. 'I thought at first he

71

was drunk or something. I mean, he was slurring his words and his eyes were sort of glazed — oh yes, and there were funny red spots round his mouth — not normal spots, more like some sort of a rash. Then, when he dropped his bag and I found the tin of glue, it all fell into place.

'Do you remember that leaflet that the Drugs Centre gave us when they came round to talk about drug abuse? Well, it was all in there. I just hadn't made the connection. So then I decided to monitor him secretly at school, and you know what? He's hardly ever there. Apparently, he checks in for registration in the morning and then does a runner.'

'How did you find that out?'

'One of the girls in his science set told me. They've all noticed that he's behaving weird as well.'

'So hadn't you better tell Mrs Hobson? After all, she is Head of Year.'

Melissa pulled a face. 'I wondered about that,' she admitted, 'but I don't want to drop him in it. He's in enough trouble as it is.'

Melanie sighed. 'Sounds to me like he's in a lot more than just trouble,' she said gravely. 'If he is sniffing glue then he's in serious danger. Kids have died from solvent abuse. You read about it in the local papers. And if he's sniffing anything, he shouldn't be left on his own, should he? That man said you could be sick and inhale it and choke. And if he's missing school on top of it, then what's going to happen next term about his GCSE's?'

'I don't know,' Melissa said unhappily, 'and I honestly wish I didn't care.'

'But you do care, don't you, that's quite obvious.'

'I don't *want* to,' Melissa admitted, 'it's just that I keep remembering how we used to be such good friends when we were younger. I mean, he was like a brother, we were that close. And he came to church every Sunday and I know he made a commitment when he was ten, I remember him telling me about it. Somehow, I simply can't believe that he's completely gone the other way and turned his back on God.'

Melanie regarded her thoughtfully for a few seconds. 'Maybe he has, for now,' she said finally, 'but I'm sure that God hasn't turned his back on him.'

'Really?' queried Melissa. 'How can you be so certain?'

'Look at the evidence,' Melanie replied. 'Why else would you be so concerned about him? After all, you don't fancy him, do you?'

'Certainly not!' exclaimed Melissa indignantly.

'Well then, maybe God wants you to be Steve's lifeline.'

'But it's really crazy,' Melissa said, 'I don't like him any more, I never see him and when I do, he's always slagging me off in front of his mates or making fun of what I believe in. I mean, can you seriously imagine me going up to him in the street and saying, "Steve, God wants me to tell you to repent, stop sniffing glue, give up all your creepy friends and come back to church?" 'cos I can't. He'd probably *kill* me. Anyway, I couldn't do it. It's just not my style. So what earthly use am I?'

'You can pray for him.'

'I *have* prayed,' Melissa began and then stopped. 'Get me out of this,' was probably not the prayer Melanie had in mind.

'And you can have faith that God will reach Steve somehow, in his own time,' Melanie continued quietly.

'Do you seriously believe that will ever happen?'

queried Melissa doubtfully. 'I mean, he seems so far away.'

'Why not? Look at all those kids who became Christians after the Chuck Faithful meeting. Yes, I believe it could happen. Though it might mean things getting worse before they get better.'

'How do you mean, worse?' Melissa asked cautiously.

'Dunno. Just that it often seems to happen that way,' Melanie said. 'Is this helping you at all?'

Melissa nodded. 'Yeah, it helps just to talk it over. I was going crazy having to keep it all to myself.'

'Pity I don't really know Steve,' Melanie continued. 'I've only ever seen the bad side of him. Maybe if you could find someone who knew him before all this started happening, you might be able to understand why he's turned his back on God and is getting into glue-sniffing and stuff. I mean, there has to be an explanation for his behaviour. People don't usually act out of character for nothing. It can't all be the fault of that gang he hangs out with. After all, Steve must have decided to join them at some point, mustn't he?'

Melissa thought about this. 'Yeah, you're right,' she admitted. 'People don't suddenly change, do they? There must be a logical reason. But I can't think of anybody I could talk to. Steve's no longer friends with any of the guys from my church and I don't know anyone else who really knows him well.' She sighed. 'Pity. It'd have really helped.'

Melanie yawned and glanced at her watch. 'Yikes, twelve-thirty. We'd better go to sleep. My parents will be up in a minute.'

Melissa snuggled down into the duvet. Talking to Melanie had certainly helped get things a bit clearer in her mind, but she still felt that she wasn't really making any impact on Steve's life at all, and she couldn't see how she was going to reach him. She had started to keep a regular check on the bus shelter, just in case he came back, but so far, she'd not seen him there. As for school – it was almost impossible to track him down. Either he was with his mates, or he wasn't there at all. So what else could she do?

'You OK?' came from the opposite bed.

'Fine,' Melissa replied, dragging her mind away from her problems. 'Happy birthday, Lanie, and thanks for the ace meal.'

'Yeah. My mum's not bad when she gets going, is she? Sorry about all the kiwi fruit.'

'No problem. Tell me, why does everything seem to be covered with kiwi fruit, just now?'

'Mum says there's a glut of them on the market, so they're really cheap.'

'Ah,' Melissa said, 'that explains why we keep getting them at school as well. I can't see the caterers buying in anything unless it's cheap.'

'What did Darren call them again?'

'Snot bags!'

'Eurgh. Gross!'

'I can't see Darren ever getting a girlfriend, can you?'

'Not unless he has a total personality transplant,' Melanie declared firmly. 'He's got about as much appeal as a road accident.'

They lay in silence for a few minutes.

'Lanie?'

'Yes.'

'Have you ever fancied anybody? You know, like Matthew?'

There was a pause whilst Melanie thought about this suggestion.

'Well,' she said at last, 'I like Matthew. Quite a lot really, but I don't think he likes me, not in *that* way, if you know what I mean. I think he sees me as more of a good friend.'

'Oh,' Melissa was bitterly disappointed. She had secretly hoped to get the two of them together, and then take all the credit for it herself.

'Anyway,' Melanie went on, 'my parents don't want me to start dating until after my exams.'

Another pause. 'So, how about you?' Melanie asked at last. 'Is there anybody you fancy right now?'

'Definitely not!' Melissa exclaimed. 'Every time I think I like someone, I remember Justin Adams and it makes me feel sick! I don't think I shall ever fancy anybody ever again . . . well, not for quite some time at any rate.'

She turned over and drew the duvet covers up around her face. The house was quiet and peaceful – she could just hear the sound of the TV from the lounge, but it was not really loud enough to disturb her train of thought.

As she drifted off to sleep, Melissa recalled what Melanie had said about things sometimes getting worse before they got better.

Dreamily, she wondered whether she was right, and if so, just how bad was it going to get?

~ 8 ~

The high street was heaving with people. It was nine-thirty on Friday night and looking round, Melissa reckoned that the combined sixth forms of all the local schools must be walking up and down in twos or threes or in gangs. Everybody was furtively eyeing up everybody else whilst pretending to be talking to their own little group of friends.

Melissa soon spotted Carly Salter from her school, surrounded by her little fan club. She was sauntering along without a care in the world, flicking ash onto the pavement and laughing in a shrill, affected sort of way. She noticed that Carly was following close behind a group of boys from the local sixth form college and crossed the road when they did.

It was great fun people-spotting, she decided, surveying the passing crowds from the safety of her perch on top of the wall outside the Kwik-Fit exhaust centre. Ranged along the wall were the rest of the church youth group, eating chips and chatting.

They had all been on a scavenger hunt. For the last

hour and a half, they had been adding up house numbers, finding red objects and collecting feathers and leaves, until finally they had worked their way down to the high street, where they had found Andy, the leader, outside the Chinese chippy. He had checked them off on his clipboard, and sent them in for a bag of chips each.

Melissa looked along the wall at the rest of the group. They didn't look any different to the kids passing by – same clothes, same hair styles. You couldn't possibly tell that they were Christians by just looking at them. They were just the same as everybody else (except on Sundays – most other kids stayed in bed on Sundays) and yet somehow, Melissa knew that they were different. She felt that she could rely on them. She felt that they liked her for who she was – she didn't have to prove anything when she was with them, and it made her feel relaxed and comfortable. She enjoyed being with them, because she didn't have to be the superficial, flippant, in-with-the-crowd girl that she tried hard to be during the week – a role that she was finding increasingly difficult to sustain.

Melissa had recently discovered much to her surprise, that she was becoming increasingly bored with the shallow, gossipy bitching that went on amongst her school friends. She was beginning to wonder why nobody, except for Melanie, ever talked about anything serious.

Boys and clothes, was all they seemed to find to talk about. It was like being on a verbal treadmill. And yet, she knew that only a short time ago, she had joined in such discussions with great enthusiasm. In fact she had worked really hard over the years to be accepted as part of the group. Now, she found that sometimes she wanted to tell them to shut up and get serious for a change. After all, there were more important things in life than boys and clothes. Not to mention horoscopes, she thought, pulling a face as she remembered something that had happened that day.

Sitting there on the wall, Melissa allowed her mind to drift back to lunch time, when she and Melanie had come into the classroom to find Caron, Aimee and a group of others all huddled round Caron's desk, deep in one of her fanzines. Caron had looked up as they approached and asked, 'What's your star sign then, Mel?'

Melissa had groaned inwardly, as this came up at least once a month. Lots of the girls in her class were horoscope junkies, reading their predictions and then trying to stick scrupulously to what they said. And they had the nerve to call her and Melanie narrow-minded, Melissa often thought to herself, but she had never actually pointed this out to them, preferring to fend them off by pretending she had to be somewhere else.

'So?' Caron persisted. 'When's your birthday?'

'July, isn't it?' Aimee interrupted before Melissa could say a word. 'So she's a Cancer.'

She stared down at the magazine and then read out, 'A day to sit back and do nothing. Don't make any plans. Nothing much will happen to you today.'

Melissa stood there feeling awkward and wishing she could think of something appropriate to say in reply.

'OK Melanie,' Caron said, 'when's your birthday?'

'Sorry,' Melanie said quickly, 'but I'm not interested.'

Caron and Aimee exchanged sly glances. They loved baiting Melanie, or anybody else who wouldn't go along with whatever scam they were pulling.

'Don't you *want* to know what's going to happen to you today, then?' Aimee asked, innocently.

'Nope,' Melanie replied calmly. 'And if I did, I'd rather ask the star-maker than the stars.' Then, she had turned her back on the whole lot of them and gone over to her desk.

It was such a clever answer, Melissa thought enviously. Why hadn't she thought of it?

Suddenly, Melissa had a mental picture of Caron and Aimee and the rest of her class mates. They were like animals in a cage, she thought, performing the same boring old routine day after day, which was funny because there was a time when she had seen her Christian friends as being the ones in cages — forbidden to do this, or not allowed to do that, which in turn was why she'd always tried to have a foot in either camp.

Maybe there were different kinds of cages. . .

Suddenly, her train of thought was rudely interrupted. There was a shout, and everybody turned round and stood still. Something was going on down the far end of the high street. Then there was the unmistakable sound of a police siren and people began scattering in all directions.

'Stay where you are!' Andy commanded, as a big group of boys came thundering along the pavement, pushing people aside in their haste to get away. It was obvious from the speed and panic in their footsteps that they were trying to get away from the police. They disappeared round the corner, the panda car in hot pursuit, and a crowd of interested followers bringing up the rear.

'OK,' Andy said. 'Panic over. Everybody off the wall and back to the church.'

Melissa looked down. There was something on the

pavement. It looked like somebody had dropped it. Maybe one of the boys. She eased herself off the wall and bent down to pick it up. It was a green baseball cap. Somehow, she just knew who owned it.

'What've you got there, Mel?' one of the group asked curiously.

Melissa stuffed the cap into her anorak pocket. 'It's nothing,' she replied. 'Nothing at all.'

'Nothing much will happen to you today', she remembered the words of Caron's horoscope. Well, now something *had* happened. Something pretty important too, which only went to show just how wrong those things really were, didn't it!

It was surprising how quickly life returned to normal, Melissa thought to herself as she opened her eyes to a dull, overcast Monday morning.

Mum had been back only three weeks and already it seemed as if she had never been away. Admittedly, she still had to take it easy, which meant that Melissa hadn't quite managed to get out of all the boring housework, but by and large, things had got back to normal pretty fast — same old requests to turn down her music, criticism of her clothes and personal appearance, arguments over how long she spent in the bathroom — nothing had changed much, except for the food, which was better and more varied now Mum was back in charge of the kitchen.

Fortunately, Alice had quite recovered from the great gerbil disaster, thanks to Michael and Madonna, her two new gerbils, and Alex had recently dumped Tasha as he said that he was far too young to think of settling down yet. Yeah, nothing changes much round here, she decided, wandering downstairs in search of something to eat.

She went into the lounge, where her mum was doing strange leg-waving exercises on the floor. Alice was lying next to her, trying to copy her. There was a bowl of cereal on the floor, from which Mewcus was stealthily helping himself to a second breakfast.

'Nice one, Mum,' Melissa remarked, strolling into the kitchen and picking up a piece of cold toast.

Her mother sat up. 'The canteen closes at eight o'clock,' she remarked sarcastically. 'I haven't got all morning to wait for you to rouse yourself.'

'No problem.' Melissa spread the toast with a generous layer of peanut butter. Then, seeing that her mum had gone back to her exercises, she went to the cupboard, and sneakily added a sprinkling of jelly sweets. It looked totally disgusting but it tasted great!

The DJ on the kitchen radio gave out the time and Melissa hastily stuffed the last bite of gooey cold toast into her mouth. If she didn't get her act together and *fast*, she was going to be late for school, which she didn't want to happen, not today. She had to catch Steve before registration. She swallowed some juice, put the glass into the sink and went to find her bag.

'So, what's your problem, then?' Steve stood, hands on hips, staring defensively at her.

Melissa had finally run him to ground outside the Science Block. Steve had not looked particularly overjoyed to see her and had been very reluctant to follow her to a quiet, secluded part of the grounds where Melissa hoped, for both their sakes, that nobody would see them together.

Opening her bag, Melissa pulled out the green baseball cap. She held it out. 'Yours?' she asked.

Steve took it and pretended to examine it carefully. 'Yeah,' he said. 'Looks like mine. Thanks.' He looked down at it for a few seconds and then asked casually, 'Where did you find it?'

'Where did you lose it?' Melissa replied, looking at him steadily.

'Dunno,' Steve answered vaguely. 'Could've been anywhere.'

'Like the high street, last Friday night?' Melissa inquired.

Steve shot her a quick glance.

'Because that's where I picked it up,' she continued. 'You must have dropped it when you were running from the police.'

Steve's face still betrayed nothing.

'I saw you,' Melissa went on. 'I was there with the youth group from my church. Remember them? So what were you doing, then?'

'Minding my own business.' Steve suddenly snapped, 'OK?'

'OK, OK!' Melissa raised her hands in protest. 'Look, I'm sorry I bothered. Maybe I should have taken it straight round to the police after all.'

Steve stared at her, wondering whether she was bluffing. 'Yes, well,' he hesitated, 'thanks anyway. Look, it was all nothing really.' He stood, turning the cap round and round between his fingers. 'It was just a bit of local bother, that's all. Some of my friends can get a bit out of hand. Nothing serious.'

'No? So why were the police after them, if it was "nothing serious"?'

'I don't know,' Steve replied. 'Maybe somebody tipped them off that there might be trouble. You know how it goes.'

'No, sorry Steve, I don't know,' Melissa stated. 'My mates don't generally get into trouble with the police.'

'Well, good for you and your mates,' Steve sneered.

83

'Anyway, like I told you, it was nothing. Forget it.'

Melissa stared straight at him but Steve lowered his eyes. He couldn't meet her gaze. Melissa sighed. She desperately wanted to believe him. The trouble was that if she went on questioning him, she would only make him more cross and drive him further away. She decided to risk one further question.

'There's something else I wanted to ask you,' she ventured, painfully aware that she was treading on quicksand.

'You really don't give up, do you?' Steve said. 'OK, what *now*?'

'That day when I saw you in the bus shelter. . .'

'Oh yeah, that. I was waiting for you to get round to asking me about that day. Somehow, I just knew that you wouldn't forget.'

'It was just that you seemed so . . . ill.' Melissa groped around for a word that didn't say exactly what she wanted to say, and found one that didn't really say anything at all.

'Ill?' Steve stared at her coldly. He was obviously not going to make it easy for her, Melissa thought.

'Yeah . . . you know, not yourself. I wondered whether you were . . . feeling better.'

Steve looked at her and smiled grimly. It was quite obvious that he knew exactly what she was talking about, and Melissa knew that he knew, but somehow, it felt better to couch it in vague, euphemistic language. That way, neither of them was in danger of admitting to anything.

'So why do you want to know?' he inquired.

Melissa hesitated.

'Can't leave me alone, eh? Have to go sticking your nose into my business, don't you? I knew that day as soon as I'd split, that you'd be after me – I just knew it. Some time, some place, you'd turn up and start hassling me.'

'I only wanted to check that you're OK,' Melissa said, indignantly, 'though I don't know why I'm even bothering.'

'Well, thanks,' Steve said, sarcastically. 'It really makes all the difference to know you care.'

'For goodness sake, Steve,' Melissa retorted, stung by his hard, cynical tone of voice. 'What's your problem?'

'I don't have a problem,' Steve snapped straight back. 'You're the one with the problem – you and all your goody-goody friends from church.'

'How do you figure that out, then?'

'Because you're not living in the real world, are you?'

'Yeah?' Melissa replied, surprising herself by just how aggressive she sounded. Keep calm, she told herself, he's just not worth losing your cool over.

'Well,' Steve continued, still with the cold, hard expression on his face that made Melissa long to punch him, 'look at all the rubbish you keep on spouting about God.'

'It's not rubbish.'

'Yes it is,' Steve came back quickly. 'It doesn't work.'

'Well, you used to believe it,' Melissa countered, trying to sound calm whilst inwardly fuming.

'Look, I used to believe there really was a tooth fairy. So what?'

'God isn't like that.'

'No?' Steve put on an expression of great holiness. 'Dear God,' he intoned, 'please make everything all right – what a load of rubbish! Nobody gives a damn about you in this world. You have to make it on your own. Sink or swim. You lot, you're only fooling yourselves. You're just a lot of hypocrites! God

85

couldn't care less what happens to you – I know, believe me. I've tried it and it just doesn't work.'

'But. . .,' Melissa began helplessly.

'Didn't you hear me? Read my lips, Mel – it *doesn't work*.'

'But you. . .'

'So now you know. So why don't you just butt out and leave me alone, OK? I don't try to interfere with your life, so don't interfere with mine.'

They stood glaring at each other. Melissa felt desperate. She knew that she should be trying to argue Steve out of his position, but somehow, the right words to say would not come. There was something so bitter and so final about the way he spoke that she was stunned into silence. For a second or two, neither of them moved. Then Steve picked up his bag, slung it over one shoulder and turned on his heel.

'Thanks for finding my cap,' he said, and ran swiftly across the grass towards the stream of kids coming in through the school gates.

Melissa watched him go. It was not the first time that she had found herself in this position, she reminded herself. Somehow, her relationship with Steve was becoming characterised by him walking off and her standing there like some dumb idiot, watching him go. She sighed deeply and picked up her bag. Why did it have to be like this? she wondered as she made her way across the courtyard towards her own classroom. And why, after everything that had happened between them, did she continue to care?

Melanie was crouched over her desk, busily writing. She jumped, as Melissa came quietly up behind her, folded up the paper hastily and tried to cover it up with an exercise book. Melissa was instantly suspicious.

'What're you hiding under there, Lanie?' she demanded.

'Nothing,' Melanie answered, trying to appear cool and casual. Melissa lifted up Melanie's arm and grabbed the piece of paper. She unfolded it and read the contents. She grinned.

'Well, well,' she smirked, looking down at Melanie, who was blushing terribly. 'And I thought that you didn't fancy him!'

Melanie looked acutely embarrassed. 'I was only trying it out,' she mumbled, shamefacedly.

On the paper, Melanie had written hers and Matthew's names, one under the other. Then she had crossed out all the letters that were the same. The word 'like' was written after their joint names. Melissa had done exactly the same thing when she had fancied Justin Adams – most of the girls did it if there was a boy they liked – you wrote his name above yours, crossed out the same letters and then counted along the letters left going, Love, Like, Hate, Adore. It was the standard way of telling whether somebody fancied you back, but Melanie had always been very dismissive. It was stupid and non-biblical, she had told Melissa earnestly, and you wouldn't ever catch her doing such a daft thing.

'I'm surprised at you,' Melissa shook her head sadly, pretending to be very shocked, 'I mean, it's such a stupid and non-biblical thing to do isn't it? And weren't you the person who said that you'd never be caught doing such a daft thing? Tut, tut.'

Melanie's face was nearly crimson with embarrassment. 'Please, please, please Mel,' she pleaded, 'you won't tell anybody, will you? I mean, I'd *die* if he ever found out!'

Melissa smiled. It was not often that she felt superior

to Melanie and she was savouring the moment. 'Don't worry,' she told her reassuringly, 'your little secret is quite safe with me.'

She slipped into her seat, and began to sort out her own books. French grammar and dictation, what a drag. She sighed, and studied the back of Melanie's bowed head. She had a sinking feeling that her best friend was not going to be much use to her, yet again. Poor old Melanie, she certainly had got it bad for Matthew. She was so serious about it, too. Melissa really liked Melanie, but sometimes she exasperated her beyond all measure, and right now, Melissa decided, she was about as much use as a chocolate teapot. But she wasn't a hypocrite, Melissa thought. That was one accusation you couldn't level at her. Nor at any of her other Christian friends, she decided. Steve didn't know what he was talking about. She totally rejected his claim that they were all hypocrites. Anyway, who was he to pass judgement on them? she thought angrily. Honestly, it made her mad the way non-Christians were so quick to judge. After all, what about all those people who only came to church at Christmas and Easter, she thought to herself, warming to the subject – that was far more hypocritical, wasn't it? Not to mention all her friends who claimed to be Christians, but never set foot in a church at all. And what about those who said they believed in God, but used his name as a swear-word all the time – something that Caron always did – was that hypocritical, or what?

Melissa decided if she really put her mind to it, she could almost fill a side of A4 paper with a list of all the hypocritical things that non-Christians did. Trouble was, she thought ruefully, she'd probably have mislaid it the next time she ran into Steve. Life was like that – she never seemed to come up with really devastating arguments until after she needed them. It happened that way all the time with Alex, and now it was happening with Steve. Except that Alex was only her brother, so it didn't matter so much, whereas Steve was . . . what? An ex-friend. Yes, that was a good description of him – an ex-friend with a big mouth and an even bigger attitude problem.

'Eh bien, Melissa, dormez-vous, ce matin?' The voice of the French teacher roused Melissa from her thoughts. She looked up and blinked stupidly.

'Er, oui, Madame,' she answered, hopefully. The rest of the class tittered. 'Alors, attention, s'il vous plaît!'

She opened the French text book, whilst Madame launched into a great long lecture about the dangers of wasting time when their exams were only a couple of months away.

Melissa buried her nose in her book and tried to look busy, thinking to herself that a telling off in French sounded very much the same as a telling off in English.

~ 9 ~

It was a cold Wednesday evening just before the Easter holidays. Melissa, accompanied by Alice, was out pushing leaflets through letterboxes. The leaflets wished everybody a happy Easter and listed the times of their church services.

Twice a year, at Christmas and Easter, members of the church went round the neighbourhood leafleting – the Christmas leaflets were usually accompanied by a bit of carol singing by the more enthusiastic (and occasionally more musical) members of the congregation.

Usually, the Easter distribution was done by the housegroups, but this year Andy the youth leader had bravely volunteered the youth group to do it instead.

Melissa had put off doing her streets for days, pleading an excess of homework, a blinding headache, in fact, any excuse she could invent to get out of it. She was petrified of being spotted by some of her more cynical classmates actually distributing church stuff in public. It was the same fear that had kept her indoors on the March for Jesus last September. The rest of the family had gone, even Alex. Alice had gone, and had revelled in it – waving to all her schoolfriends, handing out balloons, and bopping to Graham Kendrick songs. Melissa had stayed at home, in her room and had just prayed that none of her friends would recognise her brother and sister and link them to her.

It was funny the way that Alice was the complete opposite to her – she loved marching and singing carols in public – and she especially loved leafleting. She liked peering into peoples' front rooms and making loud, tactless remarks about their taste in pictures and wallpaper. She enjoyed winding up dogs by barking back at them through the letterbox. She especially loved leafleting at Christmas, when she actually got to knock on doors and wish people a happy Christmas. People always offered her money – which she refused to take, as the church did not collect money for carol singing – it just leafleted. So they inevitably gave her sweets and chocolate, and complimented her on her lovely singing. Alice spent the run up to Christmas stuffed to the gills with sweets and so insufferably smug that Melissa and Alex often felt like throttling her.

It was all because of Alice that Melissa was out now, trudging down the street, pushing leaflets angrily through letterboxes. Alice had reminded Mum that Melissa hadn't delivered her leaflets yet, and as Mum was going out to a parents' night at Alice's school, she had told Melissa to take Alice with her. Stupid kid! Melissa thought. Why couldn't she just keep quiet?

She pushed yet another leaflet through yet another letterbox, only to have it pushed straight back out again. 'We're not interested!' a man's voice shouted from inside the house.

'And knickers to you too, mate,' Melissa said, pulling a face at the door.

She looked down at the leaflet. On the front cover was a plain black cross and the words, 'For God so loved the World' were printed underneath. All at once, Melissa felt an unwelcome pang of guilt. This was not exactly the right attitude, was it? She glanced swiftly up and down the street, but there was nobody in sight. Phew!

Alice bounded across the road. 'I've done all my side,' she announced cheerfully.

'Tell you what, Beastly,' Melissa said, trying to make amends for her attitude and get extra spiritual brownie points by being nice to her sister, 'let's do the next road differently, shall we? I'll do all the odd numbers, you can do the evens — we can have a competition.' Alice's eyes brightened. Leafleting *and* a competition!

'What's the prize going to be?' she asked. Melissa hadn't thought that far ahead.

'Umm, I'll think of something whilst we do it,' she promised and handed Alice a stack of leaflets. 'OK, race you!'

Alice set off determinedly down her side of the road, whilst Melissa opened the gate of the first house on her side. Thank goodness this is the last street, she thought. Ten more minutes of this torture and they could both call it a day and go home. And with a little bit of luck, she was going to get away without meeting anybody she knew.

Alice was racing ahead, as Melissa knew she would, so she deliberately slowed her pace, letting her get well in front. She posted a leaflet through the letterbox of number three, which had a frosted glass door and a pair of brass carriage lamps and moved on to number five, which had a stone donkey with a stupid expression on its face.

By the time she reached number thirty-seven, Alice was already making her way back along the other side. Melissa pushed open the gate and went up the front path. There was a large and rather impressive motor-bike propped up against the side wall, and as her feet crunched on the gravel path, she thought she saw the front-room curtains twitch. She folded up a leaflet, and was just bending down to shove it through the letterbox, which was very inconveniently placed at the bottom of the door, when the door itself opened, and she was brought face to face with a pair of pink slippers.

Melissa straightened up. A pleasant, middle-aged woman was standing on the threshold, regarding her curiously. There was something vaguely familiar about her face, Melissa thought, but she just couldn't place her finger upon what it was. Had she seen her some-where before?

'Hello,' the woman said, 'it's Melissa, isn't it? Melissa White.'

Melissa nodded, still puzzled.

'You don't remember me, do you? I'm Pat Hayes – Steve's mother. I haven't seen you for years.'

Of course! Melissa felt a sudden shock of recog-nition. Same fair hair, same pointed chin and blue eyes, same watchful, slightly wary expression. But she thought Steve lived over the other side of town, near the park. That is, he used to, in the old days.

'Er . . . hello,' she stuttered, feeling herself going red. If Steve was in, she thought, he might be listening to their conversation. She really didn't fancy running into him just now, especially doing the job she was doing.

'Steve's not here,' Pat Hayes said, as if she had read Melissa's mind. 'Look, would you like to pop in and have a hot drink? You look frozen.'

'Umm, er. . .,' Melissa floundered, 'you see, I'm supposed to be delivering leaflets.'

Mrs Hayes took one of the leaflets and stood looking at it in silence for a moment or two.

'Yes,' she said quietly, 'I see. Well then, I mustn't keep you.'

There was something in her tone of voice that jolted Melissa out of her embarrassment. She stole a lightning glance at Steve's mum, who was staring down at the cross on the leaflet's cover. Her eyes looked sad and remote and her mouth had lost its smile. Melissa was just wondering helplessly what on earth she should do, when the gate behind her clanged open and Alice bounded up the path.

'Beat you!' she yelled triumphantly. 'I've done all my side!'

Mrs Hayes seemed to shake herself out of her trance. She looked at Alice and her eyes brightened again. 'Goodness, this can't be little Alice, can it?' she asked. 'Last time I saw her she must have been only six or seven years old.'

Alice looked from Mrs Hayes to Melissa, a puzzled expression on her face.

'This is Steve's mum,' Melissa told her. 'Steve Hayes — you know, the boy who goes to my school.'

'Oh yeah,' Alice said, light finally dawning. 'The rude one who doesn't come to our church any more.'

Thanks Alice, Melissa thought, ruefully, ten out of ten for complete lack of tact. Alice edged past Melissa and peered nosily through the open front door.

'Wow,' she breathed, 'tropical fish. Cosmic.'

Mrs Hayes smiled down at her. 'Come in and have

a good look at them, if you like,' she invited. 'They belong to Steve's big brother Kenny.'

Melissa groaned inwardly, as Alice, who needed no persuading, pushed her to one side, darted inside the house, and squatted down in front of the big, brightly-lit aquarium in the hallway. She knew her young sister – given half a chance, she'd be there for ages and would be more difficult to dislodge than a limpet on a rock.

'Umm, I really think we should go now, Alice,' she said, loudly and she hoped, firmly, after a couple of minutes had passed. 'We don't want to keep Steve's mum on the doorstep. Do we?' she continued emphatically, as Alice ignored her and continued to stare hypnotically at the tiny fish darting to and fro. Melissa knew quite well that Alice had heard her, but was deliberately choosing to ignore her. Selective deafness, her mum called it.

'It's all right,' Pat Hayes said, 'let her stay as long as she wants. I'm on my own tonight as both the boys are out. I don't think either of them will be back for ages and it's nice to have a bit of female company for a change.'

Phew! Melissa thought. At least that was one problem solved. No tricky explanations. She didn't want Steve to assume she had deliberately come round to his house.

'Look,' Mrs Hayes continued, 'why don't you come in too? No sense in standing out there, freezing to death. Perhaps you'd both like a hot drink?'

Alice looked up and smiled hopefully. You little rat! Melissa thought, funny how you've suddenly got your hearing back!

'Would you like some hot chocolate?' Mrs Hayes asked her.

Alice nodded enthusiastically. 'Brilliant, thanks,' she said, and turned back to the fish tank.

Melissa stepped over the threshold and followed Steve's mum down the hallway. As she passed, she kicked Alice with one foot. 'We're not staying long, OK?' she hissed but Alice totally ignored her and continued to stare mesmerised at the tiny fish, swimming around like so many brightly-coloured jewels.

Melissa felt uneasy being here, in Steve's house. She knew it was illogical but she just couldn't help it. She kept wondering uneasily what would happen if he returned suddenly and found her in the kitchen, sitting on one of the pine bar stools talking to his mum. And there was another thing worrying her too – suppose Steve's mum started asking awkward questions? Melissa wasn't sure exactly how much she actually knew about what Steve got up to and who with. She probably had her suspicions – parents always did, didn't they? Melissa had had to field some very awkward questions from her mum when she got back from hospital, but that was different. This was Steve's life and she had been instructed to butt out. Anyway, she reminded herself, she didn't really have any proof that he was getting in trouble – just a very strong suspicion.

Mrs Hayes plugged in the kettle and put a pan of milk to warm on the hob. She reached for three mugs from a cupboard and placed them on the bar top. Then she turned, and faced Melissa.

'So how's school?' she asked. 'I expect you're studying hard for your GCSE's, aren't you?'

It was an innocent enough question, but to her horror, Melissa felt her face going red. Pull yourself together, she told herself severely, she's not working for the Spanish Inquisition.

'Umm . . . yeah, sort of,' she mumbled.

'How many subjects are you taking?'

'Eight,' Melissa told her. Am I really? she thought, hearing herself saying it — eight subjects! I haven't done nearly enough work!

'Steve's taking eight as well,' Mrs Hayes continued, 'though I suppose you already know that.'

'Not really,' Melissa replied, 'we're not in the same sets any more.'

'Oh yes, I remember now,' Steve's mum said, 'I was asking after you the other day and Steve said he hadn't seen you for ages.'

Liar! Melissa thought. He'd seen her all right, several times.

The kettle clicked itself off and Mrs Hayes spooned chocolate powder into the mugs and poured in the milk and water.

'Does your sister have sugar in her drink?'

'Three spoonfuls,' Melissa told her. 'She's totally gross.'

'Not to worry, I've got a bit of a sweet tooth myself.' Steve's mum handed her one of the mugs. 'Perhaps you'd take this out to her.'

Melissa hoisted herself off the bar stool and carried the steaming mug out to the hallway. She placed it carefully down beside Alice.

'Ten minutes,' she said briskly, 'so drink it quickly.'

She returned to the kitchen. Mrs Hayes was looking at the Easter leaflet again.

'I see you still go to that church,' she said. 'Do you like it there?'

It was such an unexpected question that for a minute, Melissa was thrown and didn't know what to reply.

'Yeah, I guess so,' she said at last. 'I mean, I've been

97

going all my life, so maybe it's like a bit of a habit, but it's OK. As long as there are a few decent choruses and the sermon doesn't go on too long,' she added.

Mrs Hayes smiled. Melissa had read in some novel about somebody with a 'sad smile'. She had often wondered what it looked like. Now, suddenly, she felt she knew.

'Steve doesn't go to church any more,' Mrs Hayes said.

'No.'

'Sometimes, you know, I think things would have been . . . easier for him if he did.'

'Yeah?' Melissa wasn't sure what to say in reply. She wondered uneasily where this conversation was going. The best thing was probably to be non-committal, she decided, that way she wouldn't get anybody into trouble.

Mrs Hayes sighed and cradled her mug between her hands. 'You know, looking back, it was my fault that he stopped going. He was quite contented to go regularly every Sunday when he was younger, wasn't he?' Melissa nodded. 'We even used to tease him about it,' Mrs Hayes went on. 'We used to call him a real Holy Joe, but he didn't mind it. And then two years back, his dad died. Maybe you remember it?'

Melissa remembered. It had been in all the local papers and on the local TV news too – 'Garage owner killed by hit and run driver'. The police had made extensive investigations but they had never caught up with the driver who did it and Mrs Hayes had been forced to sell the family business, at a considerable loss, and was unable to claim any compensation from the driver, as the police had failed to trace him.

'Well,' Mrs Hayes continued, 'there was one day, just after the funeral. We were all in the kitchen, me,

Kenny and Steve, and Steve made some comment about trusting God in the tough times. I think that was what he said. Anyway, I just cracked up. What with the strain of losing his dad and all the business worries, I simply couldn't take it any more. So I turned on him. I yelled at him that there wasn't any God, or why had he allowed Mike to die like that. I shouted at Steve that he was wasting his time going to church and he was only fooling himself and that it was time he grew up and faced reality, and forgot about all his stupid religion. It was terrible. The words just flowed out. I could hear myself saying it all and I knew I shouldn't but I simply couldn't stop myself. Anyway, poor Steve just stood there, I remember it clearly, his face kind of set and very white. He didn't try to say anything in reply. He just stared at me for a bit, and then he turned and went up to his room and I heard him slam the door.

'Afterwards, of course, when I'd had a really good cry and calmed down a bit, I felt dreadful about the whole thing. I mean, it wasn't Steve's fault – I shouldn't have taken it out on him. It wasn't God's fault either, was it? Things like that just happen. They could happen to anyone, couldn't they? But it was too late. The words had been said and the damage had been done.

'Well, Steve didn't say much after that. He seemed to withdraw from Kenny and me – spent a lot of time in his room, playing his music. And he stopped going to church – he said he was too busy with school work. He was like a different person. We both tried to get through to him – Kenny especially – but Steve just bottled it all up and refused to share anything with us at all. He became a total stranger, he just appeared for meals, that was all. I supposed it was the shock of his dad's death that was doing it – it was his way of grieving. I mean, we're all different aren't we? Some people have to cry all the time and others hide their feelings away. So I decided to wait and just let him work it out of his system in his own time.

'Then, last September we finally sold the house and moved here. I sort of hoped it would mean a fresh start for all of us, away from the hurt and the painful memories. A chance to start again and rebuild our lives. But it didn't make any difference to Steve, he still kept himself very much to himself, though he had started going out a bit more. I didn't know where or who with. Well, you're all sixteen now, aren't you, and with boys, you can't keep tabs on them every minute of the day. You have to let them get on with it and just hope they'll be sensible and not do anything stupid.

'Well, one Saturday just before Christmas, Steve had got up late and he was sitting on the sofa watching the TV. I was trying to clean up a bit and Kenny was giving me a hand – he's good like that, Kenny. Anyway, I think he must've got irritated by Steve just lounging around, that and the fact that he never moved a muscle to help around the house, because he got really cross, which isn't like Kenny. "For God's sake, Steve," he told him, "isn't it time you pulled yourself together and started to get on with the rest of your life?" Well, that was it! Quick as a flash, Steve was on his feet, eyes blazing. "There is no God, big brother," he shouted, "ask Mum. And if this is supposed to be my life, then I wish I'd died in the car with Dad." And he was off out of the front door, leaving us both standing there, speechless.'

She sighed, staring down into her empty mug. 'I tell you love, I wished from the bottom of my heart that I'd never said those things when I did, but of course, it was too late now. I realised that to Steve, it was as if I'd taken away his reason for living, just like that driver took away his dad's life.

'Since then, he's hardly even been here – just comes in, has his tea and goes straight out again. I don't know where he goes or what he's doing, and somehow, I don't seem able to ask – maybe I'm scared in case I lose him altogether. That's why I sort of hoped that he'd got back together with you – but he tells me you two never see each other.'

'Um . . . yeah,' Melissa replied. So that was why Steve had been acting so strangely.

Suddenly, the pieces of the jigsaw began to fit into place and Melissa started to understand what was driving Steve.

'And if that wasn't bad enough,' Mrs Hayes said, 'I've just had a letter from his Head of Year – Mrs Hudson, isn't it?'

'Hobson,' Melissa corrected her.

'Mrs Hobson, sorry. She wants to see me about Steve. I don't suppose you know what that's about?'

'No,' Melissa lied, knowing full well.

She eased herself off the bar stool and stood up. 'Um . . . look, try not to worry. I'm sure everything will work out OK in the end,' she said. It didn't sound very convincing, but she didn't know what else she could say.

Mrs Hayes managed a wan smile. 'You're a nice girl. Thanks for listening to my troubles,' she said, leading the way out into the hall.

That night, Melissa lay awake for a long time, thinking over what Steve's mum had told her. Since she had last seen him, Melissa had made a few discreet enquiries about Steve's mates and what she had discovered did not sound good news. The word on the grapevine was that the gang had been spotted pushing drugs outside a couple of local schools. Several of its members were known to the police and already had a criminal record. Melissa wondered whether Steve knew this. Surely he must do, she thought. And if he was mixing with a group of kids that were doing drugs, how long would he be able to resist the pressure? Maybe he had already succumbed – that might explain his hostility to her, she thought.

Melissa realised that she was beginning to feel desperately sorry for Steve, which was a novelty, but she still didn't see how she could help him personally. One thing was quite clear though, Mrs Hayes had no idea what was going on and she was in for a big shock. Melissa felt sorry for her too, although she couldn't help thinking it ironic that Steve's mum saw her as a good influence on Steve. It was a bit like her parents thinking Melanie was a good influence on her!

Melissa only hoped that she wouldn't tell him about tonight, as she was sure Steve would think she was spying on him, which she wasn't. It was pure coincidence that she was leafleting down his road.

Which reminded her – the leaflets! Melissa groaned and pulled a face in the darkness. What with everything that had happened, she had completely forgotten to do the rest of the street.

~ *10* ~

The Easter holidays sped by in a haze of frantic revision. Nobody had done well in their mocks. Everyone knew that the teachers had deliberately marked them down to make them work harder, but Melissa had to admit, the trick worked. Fear was a great motivator! For almost three weeks, she reckoned, she did not emerge from her room except to eat, use the bathroom and make brief phone calls to Lanie, who was similarly imprisoned.

Then, it was the first week of the Summer term, though you would hardly know it from the weather outside. It was even colder than in January, Melissa decided as she attempted to warm her numbed fingers on one of the classroom radiators. This was not a particularly easy thing to do as there were already three of her classmates sitting on it and several more huddled in front of it with their coats on.

'This is crazy,' she complained, 'how on earth are we expected to work in these temperatures?'

'Beats me,' Aimee replied. 'My mum says it's illegal

to work when it gets as cold as this.'

'That's in a factory though,' Melanie said, 'and we're not technically being employed to work here, are we?'

'More like pigging slave labour, if you ask me,' grumbled Caron. 'And what do they call *this*?' she kicked the radiator. 'It's not even *warm*! Go on, feel it everybody. It's not, is it?'

Everybody dutifully felt the radiator. It was not even warm.

'I think Mr Halsey has to turn the heating off at the beginning of April,' Melanie sighed, 'because it's summer.'

'Well, isn't that great to know, girls,' Caron said, sarcastically. 'I mean, *look* at it!' She waved an arm in the direction of the playing fields, which were shrouded in a grey mist.

'Does it look like summer to anybody?'

Everybody stared out of the window. It did not look like summer to anybody.

'I mean, here we all are,' Caron continued, getting into her stride now, 'two months away from our GCSE's – a . . . what was it old Hogsbum called it?'

'A crucial time in your educative process,' everybody chanted together dutifully.

'Yeah that, and here we are freezing to death. Brains too numb to function properly. Going down with hypodermia. . .'

'Hypothermia,' Melanie put in quietly.

'I know what it's called, thank you very much,' Caron snapped, 'and on top of all that, we're surrounded by the biggest group of male morons in the entire galaxy!' And she glared across the room to where the boys were gathered chatting and playing with Gameboys.

'Gotta problem, Caz?' Darren raised his head from

the sports page of *The Express*, which he was reading with a group of his mates.

'Rack off Daz, you're a disease!' Caron snapped back witheringly.

'Ooer missis! Temper, temper,' Darren pretended to be frightened. 'Got your red knickers on today, then?' he asked innocently and all the boys sniggered.

Caron went bright pink and started spluttering. Everybody knew Darren was referring back to the time last term when she had brought in a carrier bag of cheap satin briefs from her mum's catalogue. It was her sheer bad luck that the bag had split open, shedding frilly underwear all over the floor. The boys had loved it, of course, but poor Caron had nearly died on the spot from embarrassment.

That was the thing about Darren, Melissa thought, allowing her mind to wander from the immediate problem of frostbite in her fingers. He had an unerring instinct for seeking out and locating your weak spot and once he had found it, he never missed a chance to go for it. With her, it was her quick temper and her faith, or sometimes, her quick temper and her lack of faith. With Caron, it was her so-called 'image'. Funnily enough, Darren never seemed to attack Melanie – probably because she alone out of all the girls refused to rise to his verbal teasing – in fact she didn't even seem to notice. But that was Melanie all over, Melissa decided, she was totally unlike the rest of the girls in the class. She glanced over at Melanie, who had moved away from the radiator and was now calmly sorting her books out, seemingly oblivious to what was going on around her, whilst Caron was hopping up and down, steam coming out of her ears and looking about ready to erupt.

Once again she was struck by the difference

between them. It was not just physical — Caron was petite, her thick brown hair cut to frame her small cat-like features, her uniform neat and immaculate whilst Melanie was tall and gave the appearance of being all angles and elbows. She had recently taken to wearing her long blonde hair down over her shoulders, which meant that it fell across her face every time she bent forward, and got into her lunch rather a lot. She had also acquired a pair of contact lenses, so her eyes were red-rimmed and watered continuously. Although she pretended that it was just coincidence, Melissa knew that it was all to do with looking attractive for Matthew. Privately, Melissa thought that no boy was worth all this torture, but loyally struggled to keep her mouth shut and be supportive.

There were personality differences too — Caron was sharp and witty and spiteful and just about managed to get by with the minimum amount of work and a lot of devious cunning, whereas Melanie was scrupulously hard-working to a fault and did not possess a spiteful bone in her body.

Melissa had to admit that in the past she had enjoyed hanging out with Caron and her cronies, she had liked the bitching and of course the endless opportunities to try on fashionable clothes. She had especially liked it when Caron sounded off about the boys in their class, all of whom she hated and utterly despised, especially Darren, who had apparently done something unspeakable to her at Junior school, but she was rapidly beginning to realise that Caron and Co. had a fairly limited repertoire and were useless for anything more than air-head chat in the girls' toilets. She knew, for instance, that she simply could not confide in them about Steve and her fears for him. Whereas Melanie had listened, been supportive and, Melissa knew, was praying for Steve.

Melissa sighed. Steve was still very much on her mind, as he had been all over the Easter holiday. Every now and then she had found herself thinking about him, wondering whether he was doing any work for his GCSE's, hoping that he was and above all, praying that somehow, he might come to his senses and get his life together before it was too late.

Melissa sat down in her place and consulted her timetable, which was pinned inside her desk. Double history. What a pain. The tips of her fingers had gone purply-pink and were refusing to bend. She pulled the sleeves of her jumper down as far as she could, and wished she'd been sensible and worn a body. Idly, she began flicking through her textbook. Perhaps she'd been born into the wrong time. The Elizabethans looked like fun – all those ruffs and brocade dresses. Complete absence of GCSE's. And of proper toilets and central heating, she reminded herself. Let alone River Island and a good Boots. Maybe there was something to be said for the twentieth century after all.

'Earth to Melissa . . . earth to Melissa . . . come in Melissa!'

Melissa jumped and looked up hastily. It was supper-time and she had allowed her mind to drift off again. She was thinking about Steve (no surprise!). Was he really on drugs? Or was she jumping to conclusions yet again?

'You've been sitting there staring into space for five minutes,' commented her mum. 'Eat your tea or it'll get cold.'

Melissa stared down at her chicken casserole and poked it around with her fork. She discovered a small piece of sweet corn. It looked just like a baby armadillo. How utterly gross, she thought, pushing it to one side of her plate.

'Mum. . .,' she began, slowly.

'Ah, communication has been restored!'

'Suppose somebody knew something about somebody else – like something they were doing wrong, should they tell someone?'

'Wow,' Alex said admiringly. 'Impressive speech. Grade A English here we come!'

Melissa's mum frowned, 'I'm not sure I quite understand . . . what has this somebody done?'

'It wasn't me,' Alice put in hastily.

'I mean say, for instance – and it's only for instance – suppose somebody was into drugs.'

'Melissa you're not – '

'No, no, not *me*! Honestly Mum, can't you credit me with *some* brain! I meant for instance.'

Melissa's mum thought for a bit. 'I think if it was something really serious – like drugs – it would be right to tell. After all, it would be for their own good. They could be helped to sort themselves out.' She gave Melissa a searching look. 'Why, is somebody you know taking drugs?'

Melissa swallowed hard. 'Uh . . . I don't think so,' she said, 'I was speaking hypothetically.'

'Is that some foreign language?' Alice asked, interested.

'No,' Alex told her, 'it means something that doesn't really exist, but just might.'

'Ah, I see,' Alice said thoughtfully, 'like Father Christmas.'

Melissa got up from the table. This conversation was getting a bit unreal. 'I think I'll go up to my room and do some work,' she said.

'She's speaking hypothetically again,' Alex whispered to Alice. Melissa pulled a face at him and went out.

Up in her room, Melissa got out her diary, which she had all but abandoned in the face of more pressing matters, like revision. She turned to a clean page and made a list of all the reasons why she should tell somebody about Steve. Then she made a list of all the reasons why she should not. Unfortunately, they came out exactly equal, so that was no real help.

If she did tell, and Steve or any of his mates found out, she would be history. If she kept quiet and something terrible happened, she would blame herself for the rest of her life. It was not an easy choice. She stared gloomily out of the window. What would Melanie do in this situation, she wondered. Come to think of it, what would the great Matthew do?

'What would *you* do?' she asked God, but as she expected, no divine words of wisdom and guidance appeared in the sky. 'Typical!' she muttered under her breath.

It seemed that as usual, nobody knew or cared about her problems. Melanie was in love, God was not bothered and she was left to handle things entirely on her own. Melissa felt that she had the power to make or break things for Steve. The trouble was, she just didn't know what to do for the best.

The classroom door swung open and Darren swaggered into the room, brimming over with his own importance, as usual. It was nine-fifty, second period of the morning.

'Hey everybody,' he announced, 'guess what?'

Second period on Wednesday was supposed to be

a study period, which meant that everybody had text-books open on their desks and some people were actually reading them. Most of the class, however, were seizing the opportunity for a quick gossip before their next lesson.

Everybody looked up and the girls exchanged wary glances. Darren was quite capable of getting everyone's attention only to relate some totally obscene joke. He got a great kick out of watching the girls getting embarrassed as all the boys laughed and nudged one another.

Darren moved to centre stage, grinning. Melissa alone still bent over her book, doing her level best to ignore him just in case this was anything to do with her, personally. It would not be the first time he had tried to embarrass her in public and she was deter-mined not to give him the satisfaction again. She pretended to be deep in study.

'I've just seen a police car in the car park,' Darren announced.

'So? Big deal,' one of the boys replied, witheringly, 'probably some cop's come to talk to Year Seven about not talking to nasty old men.'

'Nah, mate,' Darren said, 'you're not with me. It's not the car, it's who I saw getting into it.'

'Who?' somebody asked. Darren smiled meaning-fully, waiting until every eye was fixed on his face. He was a master of timing and this news was too big to be casually imparted.

'Somebody from this school,' he said, waiting for the reaction. He was not disappointed.

'Who was it?'

'Tell us.'

'Anybody we know?'

Darren beamed triumphantly. This was more like

it. He waited for an infinitesimal moment, savouring his turn in the limelight, before he replied, 'It was Steve Hayes from our year. And he didn't look too happy about it, I can tell you.'

There was a shocked silence broken finally by Melanie, who asked in a shaken voice, 'Why do the police want to see him?'

Darren looked round at the class. 'Drugs,' he said, lowering his voice in a confidential way.

'Yeah?' somebody else asked. 'You sure?'

'I know for certain sure, believe me,' Darren replied. 'You see, there's quite a few gangs working out of my estate. Some do cars, some nick stuff, you know the sort of thing I mean. Well, there's one group who've got into drugs – supplying them for the big raves and that. So last night there was a rumour that the Bill was onto them, which meant that everybody went underground – honestly, it was so dead quiet out that you almost heard your own breath. Anyway, first thing this morning, they were all picked up and taken in. Well, I've seen Steve hanging out with them, he's over there almost every evening nowadays, so it stands to reason, doesn't it? Shouldn't have happened at all, really. All I can think of is somebody must've grassed them up.' He shook his head sadly and shot Melissa a quick, crafty glance. 'Poor old Steve, then. What a shame, eh? Wonder how long he'll get,' he paused. 'One of your lot, wasn't he?' he remarked, looking casually at Melissa.

'I don't know what you mean,' Melissa's voice quavered dangerously.

'Yes you do. Didn't he go to your church an' that?'

'No,' Melissa replied trying to keep down the rising panic.

'*Really*? Now isn't that a funny thing. I could've

sworn I saw you two together last term. Where was it now?' Darren paused and pretended to be thinking deeply. 'Oh yeah,' he said, grinning wickedly, 'outside the science block. I remember thinking to myself, "Very intimate. Good old Steve must've got religion at last," I thought.'

Several boys started wolf-whistling and staring at Melissa who, to her horror, felt her face flaming and tears coming to her eyes.

'It wasn't what you think, Daz,' she exclaimed, 'so you can just shut your flaming big mouth.'

'Oh dear, oh dear,' Darren said, looking all round in mock horror, 'and this, ladies and gentlemen, is supposed to be a Christian. Peace and love and turning the other cheek. Looks like Steve will be better off where he's going, doesn't it? Give me a quiet cell any day. Anyway, Smelly, I'd watch it if I were you. The police might just decide they want to interview you as well. For all they know, you might be an accessory.'

Darren grinned wickedly at her and then sauntered across to his seat, well pleased with his morning's work. He sat down, putting his feet up on the desk. He was immediately surrounded by a crowd of kids, all begging and pleading for more details.

Melissa sat frozen to her seat with shock. She had already spent a sleepless night going over and over in her mind yet again all the reasons for and against intervening in Steve's life, but dawn had found her still undecided what to do. She had thought that it all depended upon her decision, which was why, she told herself, she was hesitating. Somehow, it had never entered her thinking that something else was going to happen that would take the decision making away from her.

The police! That was putting the whole business

on a far more serious level. It was out of her hands now and, as she had suspected, she felt just awful. If only she had plucked up enough courage and confided in somebody, maybe this wouldn't have happened. Melanie turned round and laid a comforting hand on her arm.

'You OK, Mel? You look terribly white.'

Melissa stared back at her with blank, unseeing eyes. 'Well done Lanie,' she replied. 'You said it might get worse before it got better, didn't you? And it looks like you were quite right.'

~ *11* ~

It had been a terrible day and Melissa was cheering herself up by having a pig-out. Crisp packets littered her bedroom floor. Her desk was sticky with biscuit crumbs, melted chocolate and spilt Coke. She had not had a pig-out for ages – she usually reserved them for those mega-traumatic moments when nothing but the worst would do. This, she decided, was quite definitely one of them.

She was angry with herself because she had not managed to make up her mind to tell somebody about Steve until it was too late.

She was fed up with Melanie because she had the nerve to be happy and in love at a time when Melissa needed her to be deeply sympathetic. Melanie had even gone so far as to show Melissa a little note from Matthew, asking her to go to a gospel concert with him after her exams. It was what Melissa had been waiting for – she had been trying to get the two of them together for ages – and she knew that she should have been overjoyed for Melanie, and normally, she *would* have been, but she found that she was unable to summon up the necessary enthusiasm, and just nodded silently at Melanie. She was lucky that Melanie was too in love to notice!

She was furious with God, too. She felt that he had cheated her. For weeks she had been praying that Steve would stop and think what he was doing. She had asked God to make Steve turn his life around before it was too late, and now, when she was all involved, God had arbitrarily stepped in, taken over and left her feeling helpless and frustrated.

'I *was* going to do something,' she muttered darkly, glaring out of the window. 'You didn't have to interfere. I had it all under control.' It wasn't strictly true – she had still been vacillating between telling and keeping quiet right up until the moment that Darren made his startling announcement, but she had conveniently forgotten that, now that the choices had been taken away from her.

To add insult to injury, everybody in her class was acting like she had known about it all along, and persisted in asking her to fill them in with all the juicy details. Caron and Aimee had got extremely cross with her when she kept protesting her innocence.

'But you *must* know something!' Caron had cried, indignantly.

'Honestly, I don't.'

'You can tell us,' Aimee had cajoled. 'You know we won't tell another soul.'

'There's nothing to tell.'

'But Darren said. . .'

'Darren doesn't know anything either.'

'Oh, come on, Mel,' Caron coaxed, 'you used to be friends with Steve. And you were trying to get off with him last term,' she added, accusingly.

'I wasn't,' Melissa protested.

'We *saw* you,' Aimee snapped, 'in the canteen, remember. C'mon, tell us everything.'

It was pointless for Melissa to protest her innocence. Caron and Aimee begged. They pleaded, they threatened and finally, when it became clear even to them that Melissa wasn't going to divulge anything, they flounced off in a huff and spent the rest of the day whispering to each other and casting malicious glances in her direction. And even though Melissa kept telling herself that they were only fed up because they hadn't got anything to gossip about, she still felt miserable. It was horrid not to be believed.

Melissa took another big mouthful of chocolate and washed it down with a swig of lukewarm Coke. Hello Spot City, she thought gloomily. She decided to add Aimee and Caron to her hate-list, because they were so spiteful. But deep down inside, she hated herself most of all because she had not tried hard enough and now it was too late to try any more.

'You look pretty gutted,' Alex observed. He was making one of his rare, quick-has-anybody-got-a-camcorder appearances at the kitchen sink. He paused, soapy plate in one hand and looked closely at Melissa. 'What's the matter?' he asked.

Melissa gulped and thought hard. She did not want to get into a discussion about drugs. Not with her mum in the next room. It would be just like her to ring the school to find out what had happened. Worse still, she might even go as far as organising the other church mums into a female posse to protect their innocent offspring.

'Er. . .,' she stammered, 'umm . . . Melanie's got a new boyfriend.'

'Really?' Alice looked up from the free paper she was reading on the kitchen table. (There were six free papers delivered each week. The local press was quite clearly not into conserving trees.)

'Is he totally gorgeous?' she asked.

'He's OK, I suppose,' Melissa told her. 'Not my type. Bit boring. He's the president of the CU.'

'Oh *right*,' Alex said. 'I get it — Melanie's got a boyfriend and you haven't. Never mind Sis, it's only a matter of time before the old White magic works its fatal spell. After all,' he continued, 'look at me — film-star profile, magnetic personality, a legend in my own lunch time.' He sighed dreamily, 'Why am I so attractive to women? It's just one of life's many mysteries.'

'Like escalators,' Alice remarked.

Melissa and Alex exchanged puzzled glances. 'Escalators?' Melissa queried.

'Yes, you know. When you go down an escalator, the handrail always goes down quicker than the steps. I think that's very mysterious.'

Melissa sighed. 'Do you think she's adopted?' she whispered to Alex.

Alice promptly stuck out her tongue, rolled her eyes and pulled a face.

'No, just look at her,' Alex said, 'spitting image of you!' Melissa hit him with her tea towel.

'But seriously Mel,' Alex said, ducking, 'I can give you a few tips to get you started. You'll be fine once you get going. I mean, you *are* my sister, so it must be in your genes as well.'

'What must be?' Alice asked curiously. 'That reminds me,' she said, standing up, 'my jeans need mending.'

'Unreal, isn't she?' Melissa remarked, shaking her

head at Alice's departing back.

'One of life's original thinkers, our Beastly,' Alex nodded. 'I'm sure she's got a great future ahead of her . . . somewhere.'

He pulled the plug out of the sink and ran the cold tap to disperse the soapy bubbles. 'Right, that's me finished for the evening.' He turned and smiled encouragingly at her, 'Cheer up, Mel, love is just around the corner. After all, what's Melanie got that you haven't?'

Plenty, Melissa thought, gloomily. Like she's got Matthew, for a start. And friends who aren't avoiding her, and a proper faith and a clear conscience. She began to stack the dishes and put them away in the cupboards.

I'm jealous, she thought. For the first time in my life, I'm actually jealous of Melanie.

It was incredible how fast the news about Steve had got round the school. By the following morning, it was *the* hot topic of conversation. And, as Melissa discovered to her horror, that was not all, for as she passed through the gate, she heard a group of Year Eight kids telling each other in hushed voices, 'That's Steve's girlfriend,' as she went by.

Melissa was absolutely furious. She turned upon the little group ferociously, 'I am NOT, repeat NOT anybody's girlfriend!' she shouted at them.

There was a moment's complete silence as everybody turned round to see what all the fuss was about, and Melissa, who had never felt so embarrassed in her whole life, found herself the centre of attention, yet again. Drawing herself up to her full height, she stalked past the curious groups of onlookers and marched into school. She was painfully aware of the sniggering that accompanied her and could almost feel the eyes boring into her back as she went. She wrenched open the double doors and let them slam noisily behind her.

'Steady on.' It was one of the prefects. He paused, looked closely at her and then remarked, 'Hey, aren't you that drug kid's girlfriend?' Melissa felt tears coming to her eyes. She shook her head violently, and slunk noiselessly down the corridor, praying that God would make her invisible.

It was one of the worst days of her life. Melissa soon discovered that though it was very easy to start a rumour, it was much harder to stop it spreading. She did not know who had first put it about that she was Steve's girlfriend, (although she had her suspicions, and they were called Darren and Aimee) but whoever was responsible, by lunch time, the story was so firmly established as fact that everywhere she went, Melissa found herself being pointed out and whispered about. She could not have survived without Melanie, who loyally stuck with her and fended off the stares and questions of the curious.

'This is just awful!' Melissa groaned over lunch in the canteen. 'I feel like an animal in the zoo.'

'Try not to notice,' Melanie whispered, reassuringly. 'Just pretend it's a completely normal day.'

'Easier said than done,' Melissa told her gloomily. 'Honestly, I feel just like Gill Porter – you remember, that girl in the lower sixth who everybody said was pregnant, and then it turned out that she wasn't after all. Nothing that I say or do seems to make any difference.'

'Try not to show you care so much,' Melanie advised. 'It'll only make it worse if people see you're getting upset.'

Melissa looked across the table and attempted a

wobbly smile. 'I really don't know what I'd do without you, Lanie,' she said. 'You've been a real friend. Not like *some* people I could mention!' she added, as Caron and Aimee sauntered by, carrying their lunch- trays and deliberately ignoring her.

Melissa was stunned by the way her two 'best friends' had turned so quickly into worst enemies. She had always seen herself as universally popular and well liked, especially by Caron and Aimee. She had flattered them and gone along with whatever they were up to – sometimes compromising her faith to be in with them. Now, in the twinkling of an eye, they had both turned their backs upon her, saying that if she wasn't prepared to tell them the whole truth about her and Steve, then they didn't want anything more to do with her. They had also said some very nasty things about liars and cheats and people who sucked up and pretended to be friends, and Melissa saw clearly, for the first time, that she had wasted her time trying to be in with them. When the chips were down, Caron and Aimee and their friends were quite prepared to drop her and send her to Coventry.

What really hurt was the injustice of it. After all, Melissa knew that she hadn't done anything to deserve such isolation. It was far worse than the Justin Adams episode and this time, there was no half-term to hide behind, only the prospect of day after day of humiliation and social ostracism.

Melissa found it impossible to concentrate during the afternoon. The day dragged wearily on until, mercifully, it was three-thirty. As soon as the bell went, she grabbed her stuff and sprinted across the playground as fast as she could. She knew if she had to face any more snide comments and meaningful stares, she would break down altogether, and lose the small shreds

120

of dignity still left her.

She hurried home at top speed and slipped quietly into the house, feeling like a wounded animal. Once alone in the safety of her room, the tears came and she lay on her bed and sobbed as if her heart would break. She was a total failure. She had not done anything to help Steve and now it was too late. Nobody liked her. Nobody understood what she was going through. Everybody hated her. She was so unhappy that she wanted to die.

Eventually, she sat up and wiped her streaming eyes with her sleeve. Maybe she would have to leave school. Gill Porter had to leave school because things got so bad that she just couldn't face it any more. Maybe it would be like that for her, too. She glanced at herself in the mirror – she looked a total mess. Her hair was all over the place, her face was bright pink and blotchy and her eyes were red and swollen.

'I've reached rock bottom,' she told her reflection. She heard the front door open, and Alice's voice cheerfully announcing her return. Suddenly, Melissa knew she had to get out of the house. She needed to be on her own somewhere, to think things through.

It was beginning to rain as she slouched along Westfield Road, head down, staring forlornly at the pavement in front of her. She was too steeped in her own suffering even to be aware of the direction she was going in. It was as if her feet were taking her there unbidden. Wet and unhappy, she reached the old bus shelter. Here was her sanctuary. A place of solitude where she could sit and lick her wounds in private. But as she drew nearer, she saw that somebody else had already got there before her.

'Come to gloat, have you? Come to say "I told you so"?' Steve sat hunched in one corner.

He had looked up as Melissa stood on the threshold, mouth open in disbelief. He was the very last person she expected to see, especially right now.

'Why aren't you. . .,' she faltered.

'Still at the police station?' Steve finished. 'Because they let me go. Because I was innocent. But I don't expect you or anybody else to believe that.'

'But Darren said. . .'

'Darren knows frog all about it,' Steve cut in. 'Look, let me tell you something, drugs are for losers. All drugs. OK, maybe I didn't think that way last time I saw you, but I do now. You want to know why?' Melissa nodded, still staring at him.

'You remember that boy Kallan, the one who was in the papers a couple of weeks back?' Melissa nodded. It had made the front pages of all the local papers – 'Local boy dies after sniffing glue.'

'Remember all the fuss about him?' Steve continued. 'Well, I knew him really well. He was always hanging about on the edge of the gang. Liked to run errands, make himself useful, stuff like that. A totally harmless kid. Then one day, he must have taken it into his head to try sniffing glue. Probably he'd seen some of us doing it and he thought it was a big deal. A really grown-up thing to do, yeah? So he gets some from somewhere and he goes off by himself and tries it. And what happens? He must have collapsed and because he's all on his own, nobody with him, by the time he's discovered, he's been sick, inhaled it and he's dead.'

Steve paused and was silent for a few seconds. When he spoke again, his voice had a catch in it, as if he was fighting off tears. 'He was only ten years old Mel – ten years old! He was just a kid. What a waste of a life! He'd done nothing, been nowhere and now he never will. I tell you, it still gives me the horrors, just thinking about it – I mean, it could easily have been me.

'You know, all the time the police were asking us questions, I kept remembering that man from the Drugs Centre saying that we should never leave anybody who was sniffing glue on their own in case they collapsed or started being sick, and I began to feel really bad about Kallan, like I'd personally caused his death because I hadn't looked out for him. And then, I kept seeing my dad in my mind's eye and thinking that the way I was carrying on and the people I was hanging out with, it was like I was letting him down too. It made me stop and take a long hard look at myself and I didn't like what I saw – it seemed to me that I was going nowhere too.

'So I decided to try and turn my life around before it was too late for me as well, but when I told my mates and tried to get them to stop sniffing glue and pushing drugs, they wouldn't listen. Kept putting the pressure on me to join them again,' Steve spoke quietly, but his voice had an edge of bitterness to it.

'It's a laugh, isn't it? Me, trying to warn them that they could be heading for trouble. Must've remembered something from all that Sunday School. Anyway, when the pressure got too much for me to handle, I told them that I was getting out.'

'So why did the police want you?'

Steve laughed. A harsh, humourless laugh that made Melissa wince when she heard it.

'Because my so-called mates grassed me up, didn't they? Told the police that I was the one supplying them with stuff. Getting their own back on me for walking out on them – yeah, I know it's stupid, but that's the way they work!'

'Oh, I see,' Melissa didn't know what else to say.

'Yeah, some mates, eh? Real pals. Anyway, they took me down to the police station and some sergeant read the riot act at me. But they couldn't prove anything and I was clean, so they cautioned me and let me go.'

'Cautioned you?'

'Yeah, that means if I do anything else wrong. . .,' Steve drew one finger across his throat.

'So what happens now?'

'Now?' Steve thought for a while. 'I don't know.'

'Are you coming back to school?'

'Haven't decided,' Steve replied. 'Mrs Hobson came round my house last night, to see my mum about it.'

'She *did*?' Melissa was surprised.

'She's all right, is old Hobson. Of course my mum was in a terrible state – they rang her at work and she had to come down to the police station to get me. She kept crying and saying it was all her fault.'

Melissa could almost hear her saying it. Poor Mrs Hayes, she thought. 'So what did Mrs Hobson say?' she asked.

'She said it was up to me to decide. She's persuaded the Head to give me another chance – so long as I promise to work and not to bunk off any more.'

'That's good,' Melissa said, encouragingly.

'Maybe.'

'So when are you coming back?'

'I don't know. Got to think about it. I don't fancy everybody slagging me off all the time.'

'Yeah, I know what you mean.'

Melissa must have spoken with more emotion than she meant to, because Steve suddenly looked up and stared at her. 'Come to think of it,' he remarked, 'you don't exactly look on top of the world yourself. What's up?'

Melissa suddenly felt herself blushing. She certainly wasn't going to tell Steve the truth about what had gone on today. Fortunately, he seemed to draw his own conclusions from her silence.

'Bet it's your mates Caron and Aimee getting at you, isn't it?' Melissa nodded. 'Can't think why you go around with those two. They stink.'

'Well, I don't know why you went around with your friends either,' Melissa retorted.

'Yeah,' Steve agreed, 'looks like we've both been pretty bad judges of character.'

'Except that I've got to go back and face them tomorrow,' Melissa sighed.

There seemed nothing left to say. They sat together in the shelter, listening to the rain dripping off the roof. For a long time, neither of them spoke. Finally, Steve broke the silence.

'I'm sorry,' he said softly.

'What for?'

'Some of the things I said. The way I was. I don't know, it was like I wasn't in control any more. When Dad went, I just sort of freaked out. And then I got in with that gang, and at first, it was OK, but then, I realised I was way out of my depth and I couldn't see how to break free. There seemed no way out. Anyway, it all seems pretty stupid now, doesn't it?'

Melissa stole a quick glance at him. Steve was staring straight ahead, and there was a look of haunting sadness about his eyes. She felt her heart go out to him.

'It's OK, Steve,' she said. 'Forget it. Put it all behind you and start again. You can do it.' She tried to sound as encouraging as she could.

Steve nodded briefly, still staring ahead, saying nothing.

'And maybe. . .,' Melissa continued slowly, sensing that it was terribly important to choose her words with care, 'maybe when you've got it all together, you might think about starting again – with God?' She held her breath and waited.

'You just never give up, do you?' Steve groaned, but to her relief, he sounded amused rather than angry. 'Look, I know what you want me to do, but it's not that easy. Maybe it is for you and Melanie and the others, but not for me. Too much water under the bridge. Maybe one day, I'll work it all out, but not right now.'

'Oh,' Melissa tried to keep the disappointment out of her voice.

Steve stood up. 'Looks like the rain's eased off,' he said. 'Better split.' He turned, and smiled down at her, and for the first time in ages, Melissa caught a fleeting glimpse of the old Steve.

'Hey listen, don't you give up on me now,' he said. 'Life wouldn't be the same without you putting me straight all the time. I still need you to be there for me. Promise?'

Melissa nodded. 'Promise,' she said.

She watched from the doorway as Steve picked his way along the sodden pavement and bit back the feeling of failure. What on earth did she expect? A voice in the sky? Instant conversion? Like Steve said, life just wasn't like that.

For a long time, Melissa sat quietly on her own, staring at the drops of rain chasing each other down the window. She thought about school and about Steve and about the way her life was going. Then, gradually, almost imperceptibly, a feeling of quiet assurance began to steal over her. A feeling that in spite of everything that had gone on, in the end, things were going to work out all right for them both. All at once, Melissa saw that there was a pattern. Life was not random confusion. There was somebody in control. He was in control of Steve's life and of her life, and all he wanted from her was for her to let go and trust him.

She stood up, feeling suddenly as if a great weight had been lifted from her shoulders. It no longer mattered that Aimee and Caron weren't speaking to her. It didn't even matter what everyone at school thought about her. She could face them all with her head held high, because she knew she did not have to do it alone.

The sun had finally broken through, making the raindrops sparkle as they fell and painting rainbows in the oily puddles.

Melissa felt an unbidden surge of happiness flooding her heart.

Somewhere, over the rainbow. . .

The words of a daft song her mum sometimes sang, floated into her mind. She hummed a few bars as she started to walk back home.

Somewhere, over the rainbow, bluebirds fly. . .

Bluebirds, she thought to herself with a smile, and God's eternal promise.

If after reading this book, you would like more information and help concerning solvent abuse you can contact:

Re-Solv
(Society for the Prevention of Solvent and Volatile Substance Abuse)
30A High Street
Stone
Staffordshire ST15 8AW
Re-Solv publish booklets on solvent abuse and will be able to tell you about local agencies who can help.

The Kaleidoscope Project
40–46 Cromwell Road
Kingston Upon Thames
Surrey KT2 6RE

Tel: 0181 549 2681
A Christian organisation to support young people with drug problems. They offer help with any problem associated with drug or solvent abuse. You can phone the Kaleidoscope Project at any time of the day or night.